The WoBBLY Kids

Raising Achievement For Those Who Learn Differently

A guide for schools and teachers

Jenny Tebbutt

First published by Busybird Publishing 2021

ISBN
978-1-922691-02-6 (paperback)
978-1-922691-03-3 (ebook)

Cover design: Busybird Publishing

Layout and typesetting: Busybird Publishing

busybird publishing

Busybird Publishing
2/118 Para Road
Montmorency, Victoria
Australia 3094
www.busybird.com.au

To all the significant others and those who have made a positive difference in my life. My mother; my Nanna; my stepfather, Brian Wilson; and my husband Graham. My children, Tania, and particularly Christopher, who has taught me much of what I know.

To Jacinda Ardern, and all past, current, and future Ministers of Education and Social Development and any other politicians inspired to improve outcomes for at-risk individuals and groups.

Table of Contents

Foreword

This book is the most practical and useful resource that I have read for a long time. This is because the writer has extensive experience in the field of working with at-risk students. The fact that this experience is as a parent, as a teacher, as a specialist educator, and now as an educational consultant, makes it even more valuable.

If I had access to this book when I was teaching students with special needs, I would have been a more creative teacher, and I would have had a clearer understanding of the issues to be aware of. Student learning would have been more focused, and both the students and I would have achieved more, in a happier learning environment.

While teachers have a lot to gain from the wide-ranging topics covered here, reading this book as a parent can provide understanding and empowerment to enhance advocacy for family members. Promoting the approaches presented here will result in improved outcomes in both home and school.

This book has the content to do what few can. That is, to make a real difference to the lives of those students who stand out, both in and out of school.

Read it, and I believe that you will be empowered.

Jack Austin

Registered Educational Psychologist, Diploma of Teaching, Fellow NZPsS

Introduction

Welcome to *The Wobbly Kids.* This is a book for all those in education who work with (or parent) children with learning differences, or for those who work with children who underachieve.

As teachers, most of us were trained in mainstream education, and our approach has been 'one size fits all'. As more research becomes available, we're recognising that some children learn differently and that our traditional classroom approaches are not providing the outcomes for many that we'd like. We have many children diagnosed with dyslexia, dyspraxia, on the autism spectrum, children with ADHD and (more common recently), auditory, and visual processing disorders. We are told that the number of learners in these categories are now in excess of 20%.

Working throughout New Zealand and Australia, running workshops for teachers, many are talking about the challenges they face in education with children who learn differently and recognising that their training has not equipped them well for this role.

My own desire to become a teacher apparently began from a very young age.

At the age of 5, I was heard to say I would become a teacher and marry a farmer. Being born in England, I had to travel across to the other side of the world to fulfil both these dreams. I grew up a troubled learner myself, and despite being a hard worker and a diligent student, at best I was a C+ student.

I could never understand why I worked so hard and got so little in return. It would take me until I was 40 to find out the secrets of 'A students', and it was the beginning of me wanting to share what I had learned. Having our children and supporting their education, consolidated my desire to work in this area.

The Wobbly Kids is designed to share my journey of learning with my profession. It is intended to give class teachers the background and understanding to identify these learners, the knowledge regarding the needs of students who learn differently and the skills to teach for diversity, developing more personalised learning environments to better suit needs.

The book provides many strategies and resources, as well as instructions on how to use them. For teachers wishing to specialise in this area of education, at the end of the book, there is information and opportunities to undertake further training, through online courses and face-to-face courses. The purpose of this book is to support teachers to develop their practice in the classroom and be mentored throughout this process.

I hope you enjoy the book, and find working within this challenging area of education as rewarding as I have.

Jenny Tebbutt

Chapter One

What is the Problem?

Very often people ask me what I do. I explain that I work in education and I support the children and young people I work with to achieve their potential. Often these are children with dyslexia, dyspraxia, ADHD, and those on the autism spectrum. For some children, our education system seems to put them off balance. The systems, programmes and processes just don't suit them or meet their needs. *The Wobbly Kids* is so named to reflect this loss of balance. The book is about my journey as an educator, recognising that it is imperative that we change the system for at-risk student groups.

Like many of us, I began my career as a primary-trained teacher. My career was going along quite nicely I thought, until we had our second child. I realised quite early on that he was different from other children I taught, and from our first child. From the age of 18 months, he was very active. I can remember waking up one morning when he was about 3 and finding that he'd disappeared. You can imagine my panic, living on a farm, with waterways and rivers.

Fortunately, he was found about a kilometre and a half away. He had cycled down to the cowshed to see his father, on his little two-wheeler with training wheels. In addition to his disappearing acts, he could sometimes be found on the apex of roofs, which would always worry the people that were around him, but never him.

I recall when he went to kindergarten and the teacher said to me, 'Your son's going to need a good wife.' And I thought, what does that mean? Basically, what it meant was that he went around from activity to activity, leaving a trail of destruction behind him, and somebody had to go around and clean up after him.

Finally, he got to school, and within three months, the junior class teacher was saying to me that he was not meeting the expected milestones. I remember thinking, *No matter, I'm a good, primary-trained teacher*. At the time I prided myself on my ability to teach reading, and I can remember writing on my CVs that I had a strength area in language and reading. I thought, I've just got to get stuck in over the holidays and do some work. I did that, and unfortunately not a lot happened to change the situation.

I found myself with two problems. The first was, *How do I help my child reach his early milestones?* The second, *How do I help myself as a teacher to meet the needs of students with difficulties like these?* By then, I had started to realise that there were other children in my classes that I found difficult to teach. I spoke with my colleagues and realised that a lot of us felt that there were children in our classes that faced difficulties. We all felt our teaching was making some positive difference, but we felt we could and should be able to do more for these students.

I decided I needed to get some professional development for myself, so that I could move forward, not only to help my own child, but also to help other children that were in my classes. It wasn't long before somebody said to me, 'Have you heard about SPELD?' I hadn't heard about them, but I was told that they were an organisation that would identify children who had specific learning difficulties like dyslexia, and if they were diagnosed, a specialist programme could be designed for them.

This seemed to make good sense to me. As teachers, we are taught a good pre-test should determine the problem, followed by quality intervention and then a post-test to measure the improvement. We decided to follow this pathway and it wasn't long before our son was diagnosed with dyslexia.

I continued looking round for opportunities for myself, and I heard about the specialist course that SPELD offered. They taught a Certificate in Specific Learning Disabilities, and I enrolled in this.

This initial step was to become something that transformed my whole career, and it was the beginning of a long journey. Along the way, I did a post-graduate qualification in literacy, from Massey University. My post-graduate qualification gave me the theory and the international research base in education, and my SPELD training gave me practical programmes and resources. I believe it has been the combination of these qualifications that has really allowed my specialist understanding to come together over the last twenty years. Together, they have provided me with the knowledge I need to truly make a difference for at-risk students (those who underachieve, regardless of the reason). I have become passionate about this area of education.

I would like to start by looking at some case studies.

Case study one concerns a girl that I met when she was very young. The fact that she had learning difficulties was evident very early on. Despite having effective teaching and support, she struggled to even read and write the simplest words. By the time she was age 13, she was affected emotionally, and her self-esteem had suffered greatly. Initially her parents hadn't been keen on a diagnosis, but by the time she was 13 years of age I managed to persuade them it was a necessity.

The assessment showed that this young lady was extremely intelligent. In fact, she was in the top 5% of children academically, but she had dyslexia, which prevented her from being able to read and write like other students.

I can remember the results of the assessment caused a substantial change in her thinking. She had convinced herself that she wasn't very intelligent. She had also felt a bit confused about why she was good at some things but couldn't read and spell easily.

The assessment gave her an explanation for her difficulties, and as a result, her confidence and belief in herself grew. She went on to become Head Girl of quite a large school. At the completion of high school, she went to university and within a year of university, she was accepted for medical school. She completed fifth year at medical school with distinction, has completed her time as a junior doctor in our hospitals and has recently trained to be a GP.

I often wonder how many children we're missing in the education system because we don't have a system that offers early identification. Our teacher training focuses on preparing teachers for mainstream students, and our profession is not equipped with knowledge, strategies and techniques for at-risk students. I also wonder how many students are not achieving their potential, and how many more could be going on into professions and achievements that are currently simply lost to them.

Case study two concerns a young lad I met at the age of 5 years and 10 months. His parents brought him to me because after nearly a year of school, his self-esteem was very low. His mother said to me that he was looking forward to going to school. He was ready for school and had been waiting with excitement for months.

Within six months he'd changed his mind. He seemed disappointed and not wanting to attend school. His parents said that he had gone backwards and some of the things that he could do before he went to school he could no longer do. The family asked if I thought it could be dyslexia that was causing the problem, as they had dyslexia in the family.

We arranged to get him assessed. The assessment showed that he had dyslexia and that he was in the top 1% of children academically. In other words, he was gifted, but also had a specific learning disability. We often call these children 'twice exceptional'.

I worked then, and still do, with an organisation called Education and Achievement Association. One of our roles is to support schools with children who learn differently, developing individual education plans and supporting teachers with resources and approaches. I remember going along to the class teacher for this student. As I walked in the door, he looked up and said, 'Thank you', which I thought was a very unusual greeting.

He went on to say, 'I run the gifted programme in the school, and I felt that he should be in the gifted programme, but all the assessments that we do at school are language-based. The five-year entry test and the six-year net and other assessments did not highlight any of his strengths.' The teacher said that the specialist assessment gave him the evidence that the child was gifted, and he could now be included in the school's gifted programme.

In this situation, we had a child who could not do what other 5-year-olds could do. He could not meet his early milestones in reading and spelling and yet he had the brain of a 9 or 10-year-old. He was bored and confused.

With the specialist assessment, the school was able to design an appropriate school programme. He got assistance with his weaknesses both at school and through specialist teaching, but he was also put into the gifted programme, where his thinking and abilities were appropriately extended. For this child, early identification made a significant difference and luckily we were able to turn around the negativity he felt towards school and get him back on track.

The issue of self-esteem for new entrants is very important. Some of the recent research coming from Massey University talks about children's self-efficacy and self-belief.[1,2] We now know that this is formed and influenced at a very young age. The research says that by the first six months of school, children have already formed an opinion about themselves as learners. They have decided whether they are intelligent, and whether school is hard. Apparently, we could ask a year one class to group themselves into appropriate Reading and Maths groups, and they would be able to do this quite accurately without adult assistance. After six months of school, they can determine the pecking order in the class and who is good at what. This is a very important piece of research, and it supports the need for early identification and appropriate intervention. We all know that self-belief is vital in learning, and that, 'If you think you can, you can; and if you think you can't, you can't.' Without early identification and intervention, we are consigning children to underachievement and disappointment in their future endeavours.

Lastly, I want to talk about a group of students whom I had the privilege of working with. These are young people in alternative education, and 16 to 18-year-olds who have fallen out of school without a qualification. At 13 or 14, these children are out of mainstream school for a variety of reasons and are segregated. Prior to becoming a consultant, I had a team of staff and we offered literacy and numeracy programmes to schools and organisations to support students and raise achievement. When we first started working in this area, we were keen to find out why students were in alternative education or had fallen out of school without a qualification.

One of the first things we wanted to look at was intelligence. Were these students in these positions due to low intelligence? We decided to use a non-verbal IQ assessment to determine this. This decision was made as many of the students had literacy underachievement, had learned in bilingual settings, or came from English as a Second Language backgrounds. We felt a nonverbal IQ assessment was the best way to create a level playing field. We chose the Raven's Progressive Matrices, prepared by J. C. Raven.[3] It is based on logic, thinking and patterns and there are no words in the test.

The interesting thing about these young people was that when we did assessments, most were average in intelligence and some of them were above average.

The children did have literacy underachievement, and they also had many of the barriers to learning that we would expect to find, such as attendance problems, transience and health issues. We also found that many of these students had undiagnosed learning difficulties. Many had dyslexia, dyspraxia, ADHD, some were on the spectrum and many children had undiagnosed visual and auditory processing problems.

In addition, we decided to look at learning styles. The current research says that everyone learns best when they have an opportunity to learn things through all the senses,[4,5,6,7,8] and that we don't have a learning style per se, as was originally proposed. Despite this, our education system is renowned for being primarily an auditory learning place, and if you learn well auditorily you tend to do well at school. In our experience, those who don't learn well auditorily tend to do less well. When we assessed these students, they tended to be more visual and kinaesthetic learners, and we wondered if the auditory dominant mainstream learning environment had been a contributing factor to their underachievement.

Another interesting point to consider in relation to learning styles is that if you have an auditory processing weakness, you are at risk in a predominantly auditory classroom setting. Similarly, students with visual difficulties, placed with teachers who use a lot of visual teaching strategies, are also at risk. The important thing to learn from this is that it is vital that multisensory teaching becomes the standard approach to ensure that all students can uptake learning optimally.

For those of you who are working in a primary setting, you may be asking why we are talking about school leavers and alternative education. The truth is, if we've been in education for a period of time, we're part of a system that is responsible for a generation of students who are underachieving. If we can examine what has gone wrong for these students, we are in a much better position to make changes and ensure it doesn't happen to the next generation.

I am sure that you, as readers, can identify with some of the case studies that we've looked at, and no doubt you can relate these young people to others that you have worked with.

During my career, I became involved with SPELD, both at a local level and a national level. I spent a few years on the National Executive Committee of SPELD New Zealand, including a year as President. In this role, I attended lots of management meetings with the Ministry of Education (MOE) and had meetings with several Ministers. I remember at one of these meetings, I was asked a question by a manager in Special Education: 'Who exactly are the children that SPELD works with?' I remember being really surprised at the question. I was so surprised I didn't give a particularly good answer at the time. The question made me consider the answer very carefully, which resulted in me forming an educational model to explain learner groups.

In any given classroom, anywhere in the world – whether you have pre-schoolers or retired people learning computer skills – you'll always have a few 'first wave learners': people who learn easily, people who hardly even need a teacher. Our job is to put some learning experiences in front of them. Give them resources, and they'll almost learn despite us. There aren't too many of these but there are a few in every class.

Most of our students are what we call 'second wave learners'. These children need good first practice teaching. They need all the wonderful support programmes that we have in school.

These programmes include Rainbow Reading; Pause, Prompt, Praise; Reading Together, etc. We have some junior school language programmes (including Hei Awhiawhi Tamariki ki te Panui Pukapuka, or HPP). We also use teacher aides to support children, and there is no doubt that the Ministry of Education literacy programmes have gone a long way to supporting children and improving literacy.

We also have a range of specialist teachers. In New Zealand, we have Resource Teachers in Learning and Behaviour (RTLBs) and Resource Teachers of Literacy (RTLits). We also have SENCOs – Special Education Needs Co-ordinators – who are set up in schools, to meet the needs of the student groups.

I am sure that whatever country you are in, you will have your own great programmes and specialist teachers.

Children who are considered mainstream or second wave learners may be performing a bit above average, be performing averagely or they may be six months to two years below their chronological age. Given all the good things we do in education, it is not too difficult to bring these children up to, or close to, the achievement expected at their chronological age.

I am going to skip 'third wave learners' for the moment and go to 'fourth wave learners'. Fourth wave learners are supported by Special Education. They are often our Ongoing Resourcing Scheme (ORS) funded students. These children often have major sensory problems such as vision and hearing concerns, or they may have major physical difficulties or intellectual difficulties. Special Education is also concerned with students with severe behaviour difficulties. Up to 3% of students fall into the fourth wave category.

On the whole, in New Zealand we spend a lot of money and put a lot of resourcing into Special Education. I accept that there are still cases where funding is needed and not available, and there are children with severe cases who slip through the gaps. However, if we look at this area, it receives significant funding.

Learner Waves Model

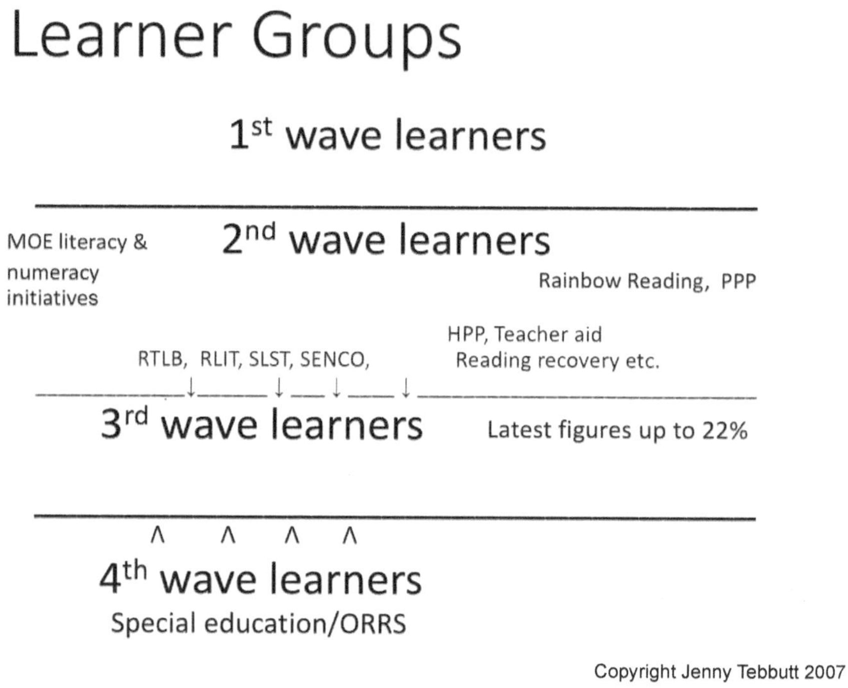

The group that we've missed out in the middle are what we call third wave learners. Third wave learners are children who learn differently. They are children who may have dyslexia, dyspraxia, they may be on the autism spectrum (which now includes Asperger's), they may have ADHD, they may have visual and auditory processing disorders.

The latest figures show that up to 22% of children in classrooms will be third wave learners.[9,10,11,12,13,14] Whilst statistical information from various sources differ, there is a consensus that 11% of students have dyslexia significantly enough to impact their education. 1% of children are believed to have dyspraxia, 3% are on the autism spectrum. In New Zealand we diagnose 2.5% with ADHD, and 5% are believed to have an auditory processing disorder. At this stage there is no agreed figure for vision, but we are already up to 22.5%. Depending on their age, these children may be three or more years below their chronological age in achievement. I believe that we have made a big mistake in education. We haven't really recognised that a third wave group exists, and we have lumped all our children into mainstream or special education without recognising that their needs are different. What we are finding is that many of these third wave learners have been through many of the great programmes we have in school, they have worked with RTLBs, RTLits and SENCOs. They have had teacher aide time, and they are still achieving well below the chronological age, often by up to 3–4 years, or more.

What we are now starting to recognise is that these children learn differently. With the advent of Magnetic Resonance Imaging (MRI) scans we can see how these children's brains function differently.[15] We now know, for example, that children with dyslexia have overactive frontal lobes and overactive occipital lobes, and they're not using the language centres of the brain for processing in the same way as those who don't have dyslexia.

It is important to answer the question: what is the difference between a second wave, low literacy student, and third wave learner?

In mainstream education, if we have a child who has a difficulty with reading, writing, maths, or spelling, what we do is give them some form of remediation that involves reading, writing, spelling, or maths. It might be with a different person or a different programme, but we focus on the curriculum or academic area that is weak.

With third wave learners, what we now know is that these children have underpinning cognitive weaknesses that are preventing them from accessing the curriculum, and these underpinning weaknesses need addressing before we can raise achievement.

Understanding these underpinning weaknesses is an important next step. The definitions are included in the glossary, but we will also discuss them here.

Most children with learning difficulties have a processing difficulty that is either a visual,[16,17,18] or an auditory difficulty.[19,20,21] Some children have both, which makes it very hard to remediate because you can't use a visual strength to support an auditory weakness or vice versa.

There are at least half a dozen visual and auditory problems that can impact a child's learning. Visual processing problems can include:

- **Visual discrimination problems, where children have difficulty seeing the differences between letters, numbers and words**

- **Visual memory problems, where children have trouble remembering what they've seen**

- **Sequencing problems, where they can't remember the sequence of events or the sequence or order that can solve a problem, or the sequence of letters to spell a word so they write 'hepl' instead of 'help'**

- **Visual closure, where seeing the whole, or a 'gestalt', is difficult**

- **Visual figure ground: for many children, the ability to distinguish the important information from the background can be compromised. They can also be so distracted by everything that's going on in the classroom, they can't pick out the**

important things to attend to, so everything gets their attention

- **Visual spatial problems, where they have difficulty using the space on the page. We often see this in writing difficulties**

- **Scanning and tracking problems, which affect them in reading.**

These visual problems are not picked up through normal eye tests, and the school vision assessments only test for some things. We now know that up to 70% of children with learning difficulties have some kind of vision problem.[22] Behavioural optometrists specialise in learning and vision. There are few in New Zealand, which poses a challenge for addressing this problem. We will discuss this important information fully in a later chapter.

In the same way that there are visual processing problems, children can have auditory processing problems.

Auditory processing problems can come in the form of:

- **Auditory discrimination, where the child has difficulty hearing the difference between letters, sounds and words**

- **Auditory memory problems, where they can't remember what they've heard**

- **Auditory sequencing problems when a child has difficulty remembering things in order**

- **Auditory attention/figure ground, where they can't filter out noise, so that if you've got things going on, such as cars going past outside the window, children playing in the playground,**

or there's a lot of talk or chatter in the class and the class teacher is trying to speak, the child finds it difficult to pay attention to the important information and screen out the rest

- **Auditory closure, where children are unable to complete words or sentences if they haven't been fully heard.**

Other underpinning cognitive weaknesses include short term and working memory difficulties.[23,24,25] We now know that working memory is one of the key factors for successful learning and if you have poor working memory, then it makes learning a challenge.

Phonemic and phonological awareness problems affect most children with learning difficulties. Most children with learning difficulties have problems with letter–sounds, phonemic and phonological awareness.[26,27,28,29,30]

Later we will discuss the research from the United States, United Kingdom, Australia and New Zealand, which clearly shows a need for a change in the way we teach reading to ensure all students are provided with a phonemic and phonological approach to literacy. The evidence for the need for a structured literacy approach (particularly in the early years) rather than the traditional balanced literacy approach, and what this means for us as educators, will be discussed in a later chapter.

This chapter's purpose is to give you an introduction to different learner types and their needs. In subsequent chapters, we will take a more in depth look at these needs.

Over the last few years, I have run courses in New Zealand and Australia. I initially thought that people may disagree with the student numbers, and that the 22% figure for third wave learners was exaggerated. Surprisingly, a lot of those in education think the 22% is about right, but quite a number think it is more than 22% who fit this category.

I remember, when I went through Teacher Training College, being told that the numbers with dyslexia were a minority, and it wouldn't be fair to the others if we catered for them. Fortunately, the research is now saying our mainstream approach isn't working for all,[31] and if we are to raise achievement and better meet student need, teaching for diversity is the way of the future.

In order for us to teach for diversity, we will need to provide substantial professional development to the sector. Mainstream teaching is the mainstay of all teacher education programmes of the past and present. The focus for all, including RTLB and RTLit teacher programmes, is based on the curriculum. Addressing the underpinning cognitive weaknesses that are causing these problems is going to take new understanding and approaches.

The remainder of this book will provide you with an opportunity to explore this area of education, and assist you to identify students, differentiate your teaching, and raise achievement for the at-risk students and groups you work with.

Chapter Two

What Does an At-Risk Learner Look Like?

In chapter one, we defined the problem in this area of education, and we identified that there is a concern regarding the number of students who are in mainstream education and are not performing to their potential.

At first glance, asking a question like what an at-risk learner looks like may appear to be rather odd. I think that many people believe that most teachers and others who work with our young people already know the answer to this question. In reality, I believe that this is one of the assumptions that has prevented us, as a sector, doing something about at-risk students earlier.

If we look at the Learning Waves model described in chapter one, we can have students who are very intelligent, and in fact even gifted, but also be at-risk learners. Having a student who is first wave and third wave at the same time suggests that this problem is not as straightforward as one might think. Also, many of the students don't come with a diagnosis, or haven't even really been identified as having a learning difficulty or difference. Most of the schools I work with say that 5% or less of their students actually have a diagnosis. While there may be more students on the radar, or the 'needs register', there is little known about the cause of any difficulties or how to address the problem.

I am able to say this with confidence for two reasons. Firstly, how many of our third wave children have worked with RTLBs, RTLits, SENCOs, have had teacher aide time and been in two or more literacy support programmes, and are still well below their chronological age? Secondly, there is a long tail of underachievers in our bell curve (pictured below). The third and fourth wave learners we mentioned in chapter one, and our Maori and Pasifika students, make up the tail end of the bell curve.[1] For those of you working with Maori and Pasifika students, and other English as a Second Language (ESL) students, etc., you will find that the resources, strategies and programmes discussed in this book will raise achievement for these groups also.

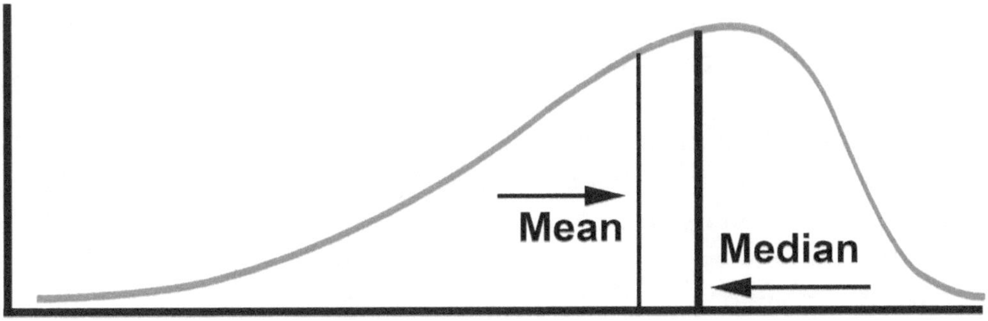

As a sector, we have applied mainstream programmes to all underachievers. Some of those who are achieving below their chronological age are in fact students with barriers to learning, which have resulted in low literacy. We have some effective programmes for these students. It is not too difficult to increase achievement for these students, to get them close to their chronological age, through effective teaching with the specialist resources and the programmes we have. Unfortunately, our experience tells us there are some students who are not achieving, despite having all these interventions. If we continue to apply mainstream programmes to third wave learners, we are going to continue to see underachieving, at-risk students in relatively large numbers.

Our first step is to differentiate between low literacy, mainstream learners, and those students who are third wave and have learning differences. As classroom teachers, we observe certain characteristics about children. A key difference is that mainstream underachievers have barriers to learning such as attendance, transience, poor health, lack of learning opportunity, etc., that result in underachievement. As discussed in chapter one, third wave learners have underpinning cognitive weaknesses to manage in addition to other circumstantial barriers to learning.

As teachers, we make observations and gather data, which forms our understanding of the needs of our students; how they learn, how they are different and have unique needs. What we now need is a process for doing this accurately.

For informal observations and discussions, a checklist can be found in the back of this book (see Appendix A). We will also discuss a screening test which we use now, originally compiled by the literacy organisation I worked with in the early 2000s. This will provide you with a systematic approach, that can then be used to inform your practice.

Parent interview times are a good opportunity to find out more about family history. My suggestion is you don't ask directly if there are any learning disabilities or dyslexia in the family, because the chances are that the last generation haven't ever been diagnosed. If instead, you ask if there is anyone in the family who has had difficulties with reading, or spelling, you are likely to get a whole different story. People are often happy to talk about members of the family who have had difficulties with learning.

Other questions you might like to ask is whether the child was early to walk, and did they crawl. The left/right movement in crawling is important to brain development. Crossing the body's midline is an important developmental milestone. If this is delayed or children have difficulty with this, and other development stages such as retained reflexes, they are more at risk of learning difficulties.[2,3]

If you are working with young children, say 5-year-olds, you might notice that some of the children take longer getting changed at swimming time, as their dressing skills are poor. You might have a dress up corner in the classroom, and you notice that they are not adept with their fine motor skills around doing up buttons or zips.

At other times you may notice that a child has problems with naming objects. They can't find the words for what they want to say, or they can't find the words quickly and have processing delays.

In a junior class you may notice that some children have problems with recognising and creating rhyme, or that they have difficulty following sequences and instructions. They just don't pick those things up as quickly as other children.

One of the interesting things we consider a marker of a learning difficulty is something called performance inconsistency. This is when a child can do something one day and not do it the next. You can teach them something on Monday and when you go to revisit it on Friday, the concept has gone, only to come back again at school the following Tuesday. Performance inconsistency is not only frustrating for the teachers, it is perhaps even more frustrating for the child. For example, they get their spelling words on Monday, and they do their weekly practise. They get tested on Thursday night and they know them. When the test arrives on Friday morning, the words have gone. They don't come back to them until Friday night, when it is too late. This happens to students in tests and exams right throughout schooling.

To make things even more difficult, performance inconsistency is often not understood by teachers and parents, and these children are often labelled as lazy and unmotivated. There is a perception that because they can do it sometimes, it must be because they are not trying hard enough, or it's a behaviour problem and they don't want to.

Sometimes these children are regarded as quick thinkers, but not necessarily when it comes to carrying out instructions. They come across as being intelligent and make valid contributions during discussion on topics, but then when they are asked to carry out a related activity which involves reading and writing, they can't seem to do it. This is confusing for us and them. It may be an indicator of a learning difficulty if you find yourself thinking, *How can they do this, but not that?* Whatever a person's intelligence level is, their performance should be consistent with their intelligence. There should not be large variations between what they can and can't do. With average intelligence, scores should sit around the average intelligence range, not have high achievement in one area and low achievement in another.

Often these students have enhanced creativity, which starts from an early age. They may have a fascination with Lego and the ability to make intricate, advanced models. They are often good with all the building toys, like K'NEX and Meccano. They graduate from Lego to the computer game Minecraft, where they design buildings and other things.

When other children have lost interest in these pastimes, the third wave children continue on with them for much longer. They often have interest and ability in science, and technology.

They may also have enhanced creativity in other ways. Particular interest and ability in art, music, drama or dance. Overall, they often appear bright, but you may find yourself thinking, *Why is it they just can't do that simple task?* They are a bit of an enigma. On one hand, they can do some things very well, but other things they just can't do at all.

One of the challenges for teachers is that when we did our basic teacher training, whether we were trained at university or whether we were trained at a teachers' college, we were trained in mainstream teaching methods. There has been very little understanding and training around students with dyslexia, dyspraxia, children on the spectrum, children with ADHD and those with auditory and visual processing disorders in our general teacher training process. Unless you took a specialist course in your training, you may have had just a short introduction to learning difficulties. Some people recall that all they had was two-hour lecture.

This lack of training poses a real challenge. Every class teacher has approximately 22% of their students (5–6 students) every year who learn differently and require differentiated teaching strategies. However, our average classroom teacher has not had the training to be able to provide for these students.

Whilst a few of these students are diagnosed, many of them are not. There is a need to have an early identification tool or screening tool that is suitable for parents and teachers to use. When I first started going down this pathway with our son in the 1990's, I was given a characteristics list that was written in plain English and did not require a university degree to interpret it. It was my understanding that this original checklist came from the Association of Learning Difficulties in Canada. Despite contacting them, I was unable to find the source for this document. I decided to rewrite it and update it with some of the more recent thinking about students with Specific Learning Disabilities (SLD).

The full 32-point checklist is included at the back of this book for ease of use (see Appendix A), but we will also discuss this fully here.

One of the challenges with early identification is that you could line up 20 children with SLD, and they would all display different characteristics. You can't say these children will always have this, this, and this. The characteristics that they have are actually very different. Due to this, we say that the symptoms children display may include characteristics from a list.

Often it is an intelligent child who fails at school. The fact that the child appears intelligent may be one of the reasons why this is not picked up early. They are often very good verbally, and they have good conversations. Thinking ability is often average or even better than their peers, so the learning difficulty is often masked by their abilities.

These children are often spoken about as having 'selective hearing', or their 'ears are painted on'. E.g., the child who hears a dog barking, or the truck horn, but doesn't hear what their parent or teacher has said. Whilst some of this behaviour can be characterised as normal childhood behaviour, children with SLD have these problems more noticeably. One of the common understandings amongst parents of children with SLD is that these children display all the normal challenges of childhood or teenage behaviours, but 'our children do it longer, louder and more often!' Whenever I hear someone say a child's ears are painted on, or they have selective hearing, I wonder what else is going on for this child.

This is also the child who never has what they need, at the right time. They forget their swimming togs, their sunhat. Their lunch money, the note about the trip, their reading bag, etc. They are in trouble at home and at school about these things. It is frustrating for teachers and parents and *even more* frustrating for the child. They want to go swimming, play outside at lunch time, go on the class trip, to the barbecue, and pools with a water slide. If they could fix this, they would. It is not a choice that they make to be badly organised and get into trouble.

This is the child whose room and desk are always in a mess, and they have a dishevelled appearance. I could almost walk around a school at lunch time and say, 'I will have a look at that child, and that one', by the way they look, shirt on back to front, messy hair, muddy legs, etc. These are also the children who lose their homework and misplace their book, or who don't know what day or month of the year it is. There is a sense of disorganisation around them.

These children are the children who don't look where they're going, who bump into doors, who trip over their feet and don't look at the person who's talking to them. Again, their sense of timing is often off, they can have poor gross motor skills or poor fine motor skills, which is one of the underpinning cognitive weaknesses. Or they can have visual spatial difficulties, and those things cause them to be clumsy. We might see children and we think they're clumsy, but we don't relate it to a learning difficulty.

These children often don't pick up the rules of socialising. They may interrupt others, or not look at the person talking to them. They may have poor greeting skills and speak too loudly. For example, running up to someone and saying, 'Hi', and slapping them on the back. They don't mean to be inappropriate, but often find themselves unpopular because of social mistakes.

One example of this was a child I worked with, who would always come up and speak to you, standing within inches of your face. If you took a step back, he would take a step closer.

One day I said to him, 'I want to talk to you about something called *personal space*.' I explained that everybody has a space around them, and when we come up and talk to people, it is important that we leave an arm's length between us and other people. If you stand too close to people, they often feel uncomfortable. You might see them take a step back. That gives you a sign that you have come too close.

The child's response was, 'Really?' It was as if I had told him something completely new and strange. A couple of weeks later, the child came up to me and stood in my personal space.

I took a step back, and he said, 'I have just done that thing, again, haven't I?' I said, 'Yes.' It took one specific teaching session, and one reminder in a situation, and that child has never made that social mistake again. We don't usually have a lesson on 'personal space' because most children don't need it.

From time to time, all of us as teachers have experiences with children who do this. We can now recognise this, and other social mistakes, as an indicator of an SLD.

Another example I would like to share is from my parent role. My son came home from school one day with a fat lip. I said, 'It looks like you have been in the wars today. What happened?'

He said, 'My teacher did it.'

Now, I knew enough to keep calm. I said, 'What happened?'

He said, 'I did something wrong at lunchtime and the teacher told me off. I was standing there, and I had a drink bottle in my hand. While he was telling me off, I took a drink out of my drink bottle. He just lost it! He ripped the drink bottle out of my hand. It caught on my lip.'

I said, 'This teacher wasn't an older person by any chance, was he?'

He looked me like I was psychic and said, 'How did you know?'

I said, 'You see when you are getting told off, people have certain expectations. You need to stand there and show you are really listening. You care about what they are saying and if possible, you look them in the eye. You certainly don't do anything else when you are being told off. When you took a drink, the impression you gave this person is you didn't care about what he was saying, and that you are rude and disrespectful. Often older people are really strict about these expectations and that's why I asked you if he was an older person.'

He looked at me incredulously, and said, 'Really?'

Teaching children how to be told off is not something we teach, and I certainly didn't expect to have to teach my son how to be told off. If we think about all the 'social mistakes' he made here, and what implications this would have for his life if he didn't learn them, it doesn't bear thinking about.

My son was about 10 when this occurred. Whilst he would go on to make other social mistakes in the future, he did learn 'how to be told off' and didn't repeat this mistake. Generally, we expect children to learn social skills through observation, and most do. Children with SLD often need *explicit* teaching of social skills. Whenever I see a child get into trouble for these kinds of problems, I always ask myself what is it that this child needs to know that they don't already, and I explicitly teach it.

Returning to discussion of characteristics, these children are often the ones who get the sequences of letters wrong in reading and / or spelling, and who get confused by the order of numbers. For example, this is the child who reverses numbers in maths, or who, in spelling words, has all the right letters but in the wrong order – 'went' is spelt 'wetn'.

This is the child who can't keep their hands to themselves, and is always touching others, e.g., they trip someone up when walking in a line from the class to the library.

This is the child who carries on a joke long after it's finished. I am sure as teachers, we all have situations we can recall where this has happened. Often this is just a mild annoyance, and minutes of lost learning time, but there can be situations which lead to serious problems. An example of this came from my own experience.

My son attended a school where he was a boarder. They had a young house master in charge of his house, who happened to be from another country and his English was not always the best. Commonly at boarding school there is a 'lights out time.' Sometimes the boys would sneak out and turn on the light, and the house master would say, 'Who on the light?' to which the boys would roar with laughter. Once or twice was a joke, but this night the boys decided to take it further and my son was selected as the person who should do the 'light turning on.' After several instances of this, the young master lost his temper and hit my son, which was filmed on a cell phone by the other students.

I found myself the next morning in the deputy principal's office, being told the story and that the video was currently being reviewed by the principal. Now the purpose of this discussion is not to discuss the disciplinary matters required, to focus on the house master, or how the school handled it. The purpose is to consider the underlying problems of learning difficulties that this incident highlights. Suffice to say, the house master got some professional development, and my boy (and the others) got some explicit teaching.

Now there were several issues here, which depict identifying characteristics of learning difficulties.

My boy and the other boys carried a joke too long.

A social mistake was made – the boys did not consider that there was anything racially inappropriate about making fun of someone's language ability, when that language is not your first.

The young person with SLD was set up to be the other victim in this situation. This is very common with children with learning difficulties, as are problems with bullying.

Another characteristic often evident in the behaviour of children with SLD is a confusion about time. They will get confused between breakfast, lunch, and dinner, in speech. They mix up yesterday, today, and tomorrow, and their timing is generally off.

They often get frustrated when they make mistakes, and they can go from zero to a hundred in terms of anger, in a split second, when things upset them. I often have parents and teachers say to me that a child just 'lost it,' and had a melt down over nothing. It may appear that way, but usually there are several situations leading up to the straw that broke the camel's back. We know the straw, but not all the other things that led up to it.

This is the child who can't tolerate the smallest mistake, who explodes at the slightest frustration, who tunes out in mid conversation. They are happy one moment, tearful the next. We'll often notice one or two children in our class who get very frustrated when they do something wrong. They often have high standards of perfection, and you might notice this when you see children tear the pages out of their book. It is not uncommon to see children who have only got a few pages left in their book.

If you work with the child, there's a lot more going on for them underneath than what you realise. It's like a volcano. There is not a lot happening on top of the ground, everything is happening underneath.

These children are often afraid to try new things, and they are frightened by changes in routines or circumstances. As teachers, we often worry about certain students on the days that we need relievers or when teacher aides are absent. It is the third wave children who have problems on these days.

Our children don't handle new situations well. They really like/need routine and they really like/need structure. Our office at Education and Achievement Association often gets calls from schools and parents when a child has been stood down. Upon investigation there has often been a reliever, the child struggled to handle the change, and an incident occurs resulting in them being stood down.

I had an example of this with my own son. I can remember he was about 12. We were getting ready for school one morning and everything was going fine, and then suddenly, I heard his bedroom door close, and I thought, that sounds strange.

He ended up locking himself in his room and he said, 'I'm not going to school, I'm not coming out.' I started to panic, I had an appointment and had to drop him at school, and we were going to be late. I tried everything, including threatening him with calling the truancy officer, and nothing worked. Then I thought to myself, something has upset him. Everything was fine and then suddenly there was a change.

So, I went to the door, and I said, 'This morning you were getting up everything seemed fine, and then suddenly something's gone wrong. Now I'm not sure what that is, and I can't help you with it if I don't know what it is. How about you let me in, and we'll talk about it, and then I'll see what I can do to help.'

He opened the door immediately and he said, 'Yesterday afternoon as I was getting on the bus to come home, the class teacher said to me, *I've enrolled you in an environmental day down at the council tomorrow,* and then suddenly the bus arrived, and I had to get on and it took off.' He then said, 'I don't know what it's about, I don't want to go, and I'm not going to school.'

I said, 'You know, I can see that you're not very sure about what it is. I'll tell you what, how about when I get to school, we'll talk to your teacher about it. We'll find out all about it, and then you can decide whether you want to go or not.'

He agreed, and much to my relief, we set off for school.

On the way to school, he saw some graffiti, that said, 'Black Drain'. He said, 'That's about the pollution that the factories are making in the area that we live, and it is polluting the rivers.'

I said, 'Yes, that's right. It sounds like you're pretty interested in that stuff.'

He said, 'Yes, I am.' He then went on about factories, and how important it is to look after the environment.

I said, 'I have a funny feeling that your teacher knows you're interested in this stuff, and that's why she's enrolled you at the environmental day.'

He said, 'Is that what it's all about?'

I said, 'I don't know but let's go and find out.'

We got to school, and yes, it was. It was actually a sand dunes project, where they were going to be working on erosion problems and planting the sand dunes to prevent erosion. They were also going to be making an environmental garden at school. The whole project turned out to be very interesting.

Despite the whole initial experience being very stressful for him, he did decide to go, and he had a fabulous day. That environmental project became an important part of his schoolwork, and he recorded the experience on his CV. It stayed on his CV until the age of about 17.

For me there was a very important lesson in that day, and that is that these children are frightened by change. They're reluctant to try anything new, and our job is not to mollycoddle them, but help them experience new things. They must be told a lot of information; they need time to prepare themselves in advance. Parents and teachers need to encourage them to try new things, but to support them in the process. Teachers will often report incidents where things go awry, and there is an eruption. After you investigate the situation, you find that the child was uncomfortable and didn't know how to handle a new situation.

These children would rather be thought of as naughty than thought of as stupid, so at times they behave badly to detract from the real issue. This is also the child who says, 'I don't care,' or, 'I won't,' when they really mean, 'I can't.'

These children often have difficulty with comprehension. They can't picture things in their mind or remember what they see.

Frequently, this is the child who bothers nobody in the classroom and does not learn. In education we have often talked about the dreamy children, who are no problem in terms of their behaviour, but they often don't learn well and fail quietly. We are now recognising these groups of children as those who have inattentive type ADHD.

These children often have poor sense awareness. They might hug the cat too tightly but can't hold their pencil. They don't feel pain or try to wear summer clothes in winter. So again, they have these anomalies going on. They might have trouble with their fine motor skills, things like holding their pencils, crayons and using scissors, and yet gross motor skills might be okay.

A lot of parents say that their children have higher pain tolerances, and they don't feel pain. I know my own boy was just bruised and battered all the time because he walked into things. I can remember once he was about 13 and he had fallen off his motorbike and was taken to hospital. He did have a broken collarbone and a chip in his knee. But they decided to keep him in because he had lots of bumps and bruises. I said he had those before he went in. I suddenly got funny looks, as if they thought maybe we beat him. But that's just how he was, he was always covered in bruises.

Frequently, this is the older child whose language comes out jumbled. They'll also stop and start in the middle of sentences, and they often talk about 'hopsitals,' 'aminals' and 'eminees.' There is usually a speech component for people with dyslexia, and you can often hear it when they have trouble saying big words. It's almost like a bit of a lisp. The language feature is part of the learning difficulty.

Frequently it's the person who's very good at something like chess, and they are a great strategist, but they can't understand a riddle or a joke.

They get bored easily and yawn a lot during learning.

They may have unexpected difficulties with some motor skills. For example, they may be a good swimmer, but then fall up the stairs. They can have good coordination and good skills in some areas, and then be particularly weak in others. This can also be coupled with performance inconsistency. You can have students or young people who are very good at some sports, some days, and then other days they're just not there with their coordination.

This is the child who wants everything done in a certain way.

They often tell tales, or they pick on others for every little thing, or they boss people around. This is one of the most unattractive characteristics of children with learning difficulties, they are often accused of telling tales on others. People say things like, 'If they minded their own business, they'd do a lot better.' For children with learning difficulties, given that their self-esteem is low, they often want to point out that they're not the only one that makes mistakes. They point out everybody else's mistakes, which makes them unpopular.

This is the child who can't keep a friend, or who prefers to play with children younger than themselves. There is always a social component to learning difficulties. These children get on better with people who are younger than themselves, or adults, but they have trouble relating to their own peer group.

This is the child who skips words, or adds them, when they're reading aloud. This characteristic signifies a visual problem.

They often see things as black or white, and don't get inference or sarcasm.

Sometimes this is the child who is slow to get up, slow to move, but quick to play. This is one of the ways that our children get a poor reputation. People say they are unmotivated, or they're lazy. Basically, when they're interested, all their neurons are firing and everything's working. When everything's too hard and they're struggling, they just get tired and can't work.

This is the child who has confusing or unexpected difficulties. Maybe they can add and multiply, but not subtract or divide. They can't do maths in their head, but they can do it on paper.

This is the child who smiles to everyone, who greets strangers with open arms, who says hello to everyone they see, and whose good nature leads them into trouble as the fall guy. This is an interesting thing. I have had a lot of Resource Teachers of Learning and Behaviour who get called in to observe these children, and they say that often the problems are not started by the child with SLD. However, when things go wrong, they don't handle it well, so it looks like they are the problem. I also have parents who say their child seems to get set up in situations to do inappropriate things. The children are often not aware that they have been set up.

I had a young man who was wagging school with a few students. They went to a disused house. They weren't damaging the house, but they shouldn't have been there. Somebody called the police. Everybody else ran away except my student, who stayed and said hello to the police. He a got charged and received 100 hours of community service for his misdemeanour, while the other students got away with it. This is a splendid example of a child who doesn't think about consequences. They don't think about what's right or wrong, they've got a good nature and won't think to run away to save themselves like others do.

These children often say things seemingly off topic at 'mat time', or in discussion time.

These children can often understand complex things and ideas, but then have trouble with something others find easy.

Occasionally, this is the child who tends to feel that life is unfair. They carry a big chip on their shoulder, and they refuse to try. Fortunately, not too many children have this characteristic. However, I do find that when children do have a chip on their shoulder and say I've got dyslexia, or I've got this, or I've got that, or I can't do this because of that, it's a tough idea to change.

These characteristics make it easier for parents and teachers to identify children with learning difficulties. It is important that we look for a cluster of symptoms. Any child or person can have one or two of the characteristics. Six or more characteristics are suggestive that further assessment may be required.

In my experience, if a child has moderate learning difficulties, they have a lot of these characteristics. The checklist is a very useful tool to use as a first step if a child has come to your attention (see Appendix A). The important thing for us to understand from this checklist, as teachers, is that often we see behaviours as part of a child's personality rather than a characteristic of a learning difficulty. By understanding what is behind behaviours, we can begin to understand the child, which will lay the foundation to meet their needs more effectively.

In chapter one, we have identified the learning and teaching problem.

In chapter two, we have discovered the characteristics of an at-risk learner.

In chapter three, we will be talking about what it feels like to be an at-risk learner.

Screening assessments will be discussed in a later chapter.

Chapter Three

What Does It Feel Like to Be an At-Risk Learner?

For many of us, as teachers, unless we have had a direct experience with either having learning difficulties ourselves or knowing someone very close to us that has, it is difficult to understand what challenges they face.

I have a colleague, who has become a close friend, who used to say to me that she had a friend with a son who she saw as a typical boy. I really respected her as a teacher, and she had three boys of her own. She was also amazing with challenging students. Surprisingly, she said she went to stay with this family for a few days and she said it was then she realised this boy was different. It wasn't until she stayed in the family home that she saw it.

This conversation made me realise that many people, even good teachers, may not pick up on learning needs and differences easily. We often talk about SLD as the hidden disability. Because children look normal and they have some great strengths, we don't easily see the problem areas so readily.

It is very common for students with SLD to be behind their peers emotionally.[1] We may have a 12-year-old who acts more like a 9- to 10-year-old, or a 15-year-old that acts more like a 12- to 13-year-old. This can continue until quite late in life.

With new research on brain development, it is recognised that cognitive function is not fully mature until well in the 20s, particularly in males.[1] I work with several clients in their twenties who are still exhibiting teenage behaviour. The negative implications this has on their lives, right from an early age, is profound. If we are to raise achievement and improve outcomes for this group, this needs addressing.

I want to give you the experience of what it feels like to be an at-risk learner. We are going to do several activities. Firstly, I'm going to direct you to the back of the book, where I've put a reading task for you (see Appendix B).

This reading task does make sense. It is a real piece of reading. Because I am a good teacher, I am going to give you some guidelines as to how you might approach the reading.

Often people with learning difficulties and visual difficulties skip words and miss lines. They will even tell you that words move and that sometimes they must catch words to read them.

You will notice when you look at the reading, that there are two lines and then a gap. If you run these two lines together and make the two lines into one line, you will be able to read it.

You have also probably heard that people with dyslexia have reversals, and they often get their 'b's and 'd's mixed up. They confuse their 'q's and 'p's, also their 'n's and 'u's, and so on.

As you're reading this text, you must think that every 'b', 'p', 'q', or 'd' could be any of these letters. You have to decide what the letter actually is.

I want you to take your time, and I want you to read through the entire text. It will take a while. When you have finished come back to this page.

How did you feel?

When I'm working with people in seminars and we complete this exercise, people say they felt really frustrated, confused, quite dumb, and by the end of it, tired. Some say it hurts their eyes. When I get people to read this aloud, they often sound like 5-year-old readers.

Usually when I am working with a group, before we start, I say that I am going to give them a couple of minutes to have a look at this text first, so it becomes a seen text.

Now as you can see, it doesn't make much difference whether this is a seen text or not. If you have trouble with it, you'll have trouble with it. When I do this in a group setting, we have some people who just give up, and we have some people who continue to try. Generally, in a group, we have a couple of first wave learners who cotton on to the pattern quite quickly. We have others who take a while, and we have another group who just don't get it at all. This experience is reflective of the first, second and third wave learners' philosophy.

I then say, 'If reading was like this for you all the time, and it never became any easier, would you enjoy reading and want to read for pleasure? Probably not, and yet we aim, in education, to instil the love of reading in all students.'

For children who have visual problems and children with phonemic/phonological awareness problems, decoding never comes easy. Because children are spending so much of their effort on decoding, they don't have any brain capacity left to comprehend, or to tell you what the story was about.

If I asked you now if you are ready for a comprehension test on this material, would you be happy about it and able to do it? Likely not.

Many teachers I work with on this task find this a really illuminating exercise. When you read well, you tend not to consider what it is like for people who have reading difficulties. This experience was designed to give you the understanding of what it is like to have a learning difficulty. The chances are that most of you reading this don't have a reading difficulty. Even if you do, you didn't have to do this exercise in public, so it wasn't embarrassing.

In a class, the student often feels they are the only one who reads badly, and this is very upsetting for them. Because being able to read and write is so fundamental to all subjects, we continue to make students face this problem daily. There are usually several students with these kinds of difficulties in a class, but because they become so good at hiding it, other students may not be aware how big the problem is.

This experience is painful for these students. The pain goes on for a very long time, and having this problem impacts every area of the curriculum and creates underachievement. Is it any wonder that as children get older, their frustration, attitude and behaviour problems increase to sometimes intolerable levels?

For our next activity, I would like you to turn to Appendix C, where you will see a star. For this activity you will need a pen and a mirror.

I would like you to trace between the lines inside the star, just by looking in the mirror. Do not look directly at the page.

Basically, what we are doing is making your brain confused. Do this activity now and then come back to this page.

You will notice you had some left/right brain confusions. Your brain wanted to go one way and your hand told you to go the other way. Wasn't it hard to turn a corner? Once you went off the line, wasn't it hard to get back on?

The reason I got you to do this activity is because I wanted you to experience what it's like to have a confused brain. For children with SLD, this is an experience that is very familiar to them.

If we compare this activity to classroom handwriting, we can start to see why children have difficulty. Children with visual problems have difficulty transferring their eyes from board to book efficiently. If the student has poor working memory, they must copy letter by letter, whereas we can retain a whole sentence. When I was first a teacher in junior classes, teaching handwriting, I could not understand why some children couldn't complete their handwriting like everybody else. I used to think it was 'only copying,' and I would keep them in at playtime to make them finish. I now owe those children an apology because I understand what was happening for them.

Children with SLD should not be copying from a board. They should have their handwriting and notes beside them. Children with SLD should also not be expected to note take.

Firstly, it takes them too long to complete it. Secondly, they don't learn anything from it because they can't take in the material.

Children with SLD cannot do more than one cognitive thing at a time. They either write notes or think but can't do both. Class teachers are best to give a child the notes and set them an activity to work with the notes, to focus on comprehension while the others are copying. The rest of the students may learn and take in the information while they are copying, so it may still be a worthwhile activity.

In summary, it is very important for us to understand how confusing it is for students who have a specific learning difficulty.

Finally, I would like to turn your attention to a YouTube clip to have a look at.[2]

www.youtube.com/watch?v=rhygmurIgG0&feature=youtu.be/

The YouTube clip is by Elliott de Neve. I think he was around 14 years of age when he made this clip, and I've been showing it at all the seminars I run around New Zealand and Australia. Elliott wants us to understand what it's like to be dyslexic and to be working in the school system.

Go ahead and look at the clip now and then come back to this page.

There are two key things that I think this clip has to teach us:

- **That people with SLD have strengths, and that often school focuses on weaknesses not strengths. The strengths that Elliot has are music, film making, computer skills, communication, and good self-esteem to name a few.**

- **Elliot highlights many people in the world with learning difficulties (dyslexia, ADHD, those on the spectrum) who are very successful, and his message is that these learning difficulties don't have to hold you back.**

Many of the successful 'greats' say they did two things. Firstly, they found their passion and worked in their area of strength. Secondly, they found people to support them and assist in their weak areas.

Sadly, today the statistics show that those with various learning difficulties are over-represented in many of society's negative statistics.[3] More of these students are included in stand-downs, suspensions and exclusions. Social workers and school counsellors see more of them. They are over-represented at a youth justice level, and they have more drug and alcohol related issues. Left unsupported, they have more mental health problems, and our prisons are filled with people with learning disabilities and those with low literacy.

The longitudinal study done in Dunedin, which followed 1000 children from birth to adulthood, also has some interesting things to say about students in at-risk groups and those with underpinning cognitive weaknesses, such as short term and working memory, executive functioning and organisational skills.[4]

Martin Westwell delivered a paper at the 2013 Acer conference.[5]

Westwell's study found that the extent to which young people have developed executive functions has been shown to profoundly affect their outcomes in terms of education, health, income and criminal behaviour.

This study confirms the consequences of an education system that does not meet the needs of at-risk groups.

Our role, I believe, is to discover how we can, as teachers, educators in the sector and others who work with young people, assist the children we come in contact with to move away from the negative side of the ledger to the positive side of the ledger.

I want you to imagine this scenario.

You woke up this morning, and the minute you opened your eyes you knew it wasn't a good day. You heard the kids shouting, you realised that you'd slept in, and you were late for work. You got up and you seemed to struggle to get through the morning, get the kids ready, get everybody out the door and get where you needed to be.

On the way to work, you were quite uncoordinated and while you were driving you cut someone off and you nearly had an accident. You got to work late, and you remembered that there was a meeting, and that you were supposed to be presenting at that meeting.

You weren't quite as prepared as you normally are. You weren't your eloquent self, and you seemed to get offside with one or two of your colleagues. Come morning teatime, you found that the people that you normally had coffee with didn't want to sit with you. You went about your day, had a few meetings or classes and then you realised that you'd forgotten one of your lesson plans and left it at home. You also realised that you had a staff meeting after school, and you weren't going to get home until 5:30 pm, and by the time you got to the staff meeting, you had a headache and just wanted to go home. Basically, your entire day didn't go well.

Now what I'd like to ask you is: If this was your reality, and if every day that you went to your workplace you experienced these things; how long would you stay in a job like this?

I've asked this question often at seminars and the overwhelming response is not very long.

Children go off to school from the age of 5 or 6, depending on which country you're in. We consign our children to attend school until at least the age of 15 years, but maybe up to 18 years. We expect children to go to school every day, with reading and writing difficulties, with a smile on their face, knowing this is at least a ten-year process. At times we may even say, 'What's wrong with you? Put a smile on your face!'

We wouldn't choose to work in a workplace that brought out all our weaknesses, and made life very difficult for us, and yet we consign children to school and expect them to do this every day for years and be happy about it.

I have also had many children in their first year of school recognise and say they are different. I have even had students who I would say are depressed and sad because they feel they don't fit in. Tragically there are even a few children who have suicidal thoughts from a very young age.

What I want you to take from this chapter is an understanding of what it feels like to be an at-risk learner and have to go through a school system when you have these difficulties. To recognise that when we have this understanding, we can work from a different perspective. To start identifying students' strengths and their needs, and to look at ways we can differentiate our teaching to improve not only outcomes for these students, but to make school a more fun place to be.

Chapter Four

What Difference Will Teaching for Diversity Make?

In the past our educational approach has been to cater for mainstream. When we teach for diversity, we cater for the needs of many different groups. Teaching for diversity considers differing home backgrounds, it cuts across socio-economic boundaries, it considers the children with learning differences, difficulties and disabilities. The research also shows that when we cater for diversity, it supports gifted children as well,[1] and includes children of different ethnicities and children who have English as a second language. There have been a lot of recent studies showing lower achievement of boys in education, and when we teach for diversity, it equalises the opportunity for all student groups.

The best evidence synthesis research has found that teaching that is responsive to diversity has a positive impact on low and high achievers at the same time.[1]

The door is now open for 'dyslexia-friendly', dyslexia-aware thinking to begin to take hold and allow change. The original work in this area came from Neil Mackay, the British dyslexia specialist.[2] He coined the term 'dyslexia-friendly schools'. In Britain, many of the local UK educational authorities took up the initiative, and they set up dyslexia-friendly schools and Good Practice Guides to better cater for students with dyslexia.

In New Zealand, the Dyslexia Foundation of New Zealand was inspired by this model, and they set up 4D Best Practice schools. There are several advantages for schools who adopt this model. In schools that operate dyslexia-friendly or dyslexia-aware policies and practices, their response times for children with dyslexia improve, and children are identified and referred much earlier. In the case study we looked at regarding school leavers in chapter one, we identified that many children currently remain undiagnosed right throughout the school system and go into adult lives without having difficulties identified and addressed.

In British schools, they also found that where schools developed policy and practice, most of these schools initially sought to contract, train, or employ a qualified dyslexia specialist within their school. One of the challenges we've had in New Zealand, which has also been discussed when I've worked in Australia, is that our teachers are not trained to work with students in at-risk groups such as students with dyslexia, dyspraxia, children on the spectrum, those with ADHD, and children with auditory and visual processing disorders, etc. To adequately support these students, a starting point is that each school requires someone specialised in this area. If we consider that 22% of a student roll fits this cohort, in a school of 500 students, approximately 110 students will benefit, and in a school with 1000 students, we are looking at 220 students. This means that every class teacher is likely to have at least five at-risk students in their care each year. If we consider the implications of this, it makes sense that we need to provide professional development for every classroom teacher. Without the development of differentiated teaching approaches and catering for the needs of at-risk learner groups, we are not providing equity in educational opportunity.

The discussion around problems related to at-risk groups, underachievement, and inequity in the education system, has been gaining a greater profile in education over the last few years. Whilst there is now little doubt that at-risk groups have been marginalised through a mainstream education approach, it is my belief that we have always done the best we can with the knowledge we have got. Over the last few years, with more recent brain research and understanding through Magnetic Resonance Imaging (MRI) scans and knowledge about research, like neuroplasticity (where neurons can be developed and strengthened), we are in a much better position to understand the problem and to make changes.[3] The failure of the educational system to deliver good outcomes and support at-risk students in the past is bad enough. To not learn from new knowledge, science and research and implement change as a result, goes against many of the values we subscribe to, at a national and international level.

Our National Administration Guidelines, or NAGs (2017 revision),[4] spell out the intentions of the sector. They have a lot to say on the topics we are discussing, and I have italicised the particularly relevant sections in NAG 1 below.

Each board, through the principal and staff, is required to:

a) develop and implement teaching and learning programmes:

    i) to provide all students in years 1–10 with opportunities to progress and achieve for success in all areas of The National Curriculum;

    ii) giving priority to *student progress and achievement in literacy and numeracy* and/or te reo matatini and pāngarau, especially in years 1–8;

    iii) giving priority to regular quality physical activity that develops movement skills for all students, especially in years 1–6;

b) through the *analysis of good quality assessment information*, evaluate the progress and achievement of students,* giving priority first to:

i) *student progress and achievement in literacy and numeracy* and / or Te Reo Matatini and pāngarau, especially in years 1–8; and then to:

ii) breadth and depth of learning related to the needs, abilities and interests of students, the nature of the school's curriculum, and the scope of The National Curriculum, as expressed in The New Zealand Curriculum 2007 or Te Marautanga o Aotearoa;

c) through the *analysis of good quality assessment information**, *identify students and groups of students*:

i) who are *not progressing and/or achieving;*

ii) who are *at risk of not progressing and/or achieving;*

iii) who have *special needs (including gifted and talented students)*; and

iv) aspects of the curriculum which require particular attention;

d) *develop and implement teaching and learning strategies* to *address the needs of students and aspects of the curriculum* identified in (c) above;

e) in consultation with the school's Māori community, develop and make known to the school's community policies, plans and targets for improving the progress and achievement of Māori students; and

f) provide appropriate career education and guidance for all students in year 7 and above, with a particular emphasis on specific career guidance for those students who have been identified by the school as being at risk of leaving school unprepared for the transition to the workplace or further education/training.

* Good quality assessment information draws on a range of evidence to evaluate the progress and achievement of students and build a comprehensive picture of student learning across the curriculum.

In addition to this, a number of the National Educational Goals (NEGs) reinforce our intentions to support at-risk student groups.[5]

NEG 1

The highest standards of achievement, through programmes which enable all students to realise their full potential as individuals, and to develop the values needed to become full members of New Zealand's society.

NEG 2

Equality of educational opportunity for all New Zealanders, by identifying and removing barriers to achievement.

NEG 4

A sound foundation in the early years for future learning and achievement through programmes which include support for parents in their vital role as their children's first teachers.

NEG 5

A broad education through a balanced curriculum covering essential learning areas. Priority should be given to the development of high levels of competence (knowledge and skills) in literacy and numeracy, science and technology and physical activity.

NEG 6

Excellence achieved through the establishment of clear learning objectives, monitoring student performance against those objectives, and programmes to meet individual need.

NEG 7

Success in their learning for those with special needs by ensuring that they are identified and receive appropriate support.

Looking at what is happening in our schools in relation to the long tail of underachievement and the numbers of students at risk in education, including the 22% that we would classify as third wave learners, I think we would be hard pressed to say that we were living up to the values in these documents for at-risk groups. Recent research has given us additional information, and with the benefit of hindsight, we now have an obligation to make changes in education to offer equity and improve outcomes and educational achievement for all groups, and not just serve well the mainstream student population that we have catered for in the past.

UN News published an article about the United Nations guidelines – technically referred to as a General Comment –[6] which provides guidance for the 166 States that have ratified the Convention on meeting their obligations under Article 24. Under this Article, it is stated that, 'Parties shall ensure an inclusive education system at all levels and life-long learning.'

In the UN News article,[6] Ms Cisternas Reys said that, 'Enabling inclusive education requires an in-depth transformation of education systems in legislation, policy and the way education is financed, administered, designed, taught and monitored ... We hope our General Comment will guide and aid States toward achieving this goal.' The UN News article, summarising the document, states that placing students with disabilities in mainstream classes without accompanying structural changes to organisation, curriculum and teaching and learning strategies, does not constitute inclusion.

The article goes on to describe inclusive education as focused on the 'full and effective participation, accessibility, attendance and achievement of all students, especially those who, for different reasons, are excluded or at risk of being marginalised.'[6]

The whole education system, from the methods to the assessments to the services, must be accessible. This includes both state-run and private schools. Legislation, policy and the design, financing, administration, and monitoring of education systems must all undergo a shift.

One of the challenges related to not having trained staff in our schools means that we have long waiting lists for support services, such as Resource Teachers of Learning and Behaviour (RTLB), Resource Teachers of Literacy (RTLit), Speech Language Therapists and Occupational Therapists, etc. There is always more need than there are resources, and consequently many children are not receiving support. If we were able to train all our teaching staff and we had a specialist in each school, such as a trained SENCO or Learning Support Co-ordinator, we would be able to deal with all the mild and moderate needs ourselves and refer on for the high-need cases only. This would ensure more student need was met at a classroom and school level, and free up the specialist services to deal with high-needs students only.

When schools are equipped to deal with at-risk students through early identification and provision, not only do they reduce the load on specialist resources, but they also save money. It is widely recognised that children who have learning difficulties often develop learned helplessness, and they also have poor strategies for learning. The longer children are left with undiagnosed and unsupported problems, the more ingrained poor strategies and learned helplessness becomes, which then requires greater remediation at greater cost. Through early identification, addressing underpinning cognitive weaknesses and teaching effective metacognitive strategies, we can raise achievement, improve outcomes, and reduce the time and therefore cost of ongoing intervention.

One of the important things about the Dyslexia Foundation and the 4D philosophy is that it advocates for a focus on whole school improvement through raising the achievement of vulnerable learners.[7] This fits with a lot of the research in professional development, which recognises that whilst it is beneficial for people to go on courses individually, it is even more beneficial – and most change occurs – when a whole school approach or a whole school focus is undertaken.

The 4D approach says, 'If we get it right for dyslexia, then we get it right for all.'

As I travel around New Zealand, and when I am working with schools in Australia, I've noticed schools are not only looking at the needs of those with dyslexia, but also looking at the wider needs of at-risk groups. If we embark on a 4D approach, we can extend this thinking to the needs of all at-risk students and be confident that we are making a positive difference to all underachieving groups.

4D invests in teachers as a solution, rather than products or software packages.

There has been a danger and a tendency for schools, and people, who don't have the knowledge or experience regarding children with learning difficulties, to over-focus on products or software packages.

Whilst there are many good products and software packages out there which can enhance achievement, they are only part of an effective programme and effective teaching. Later, we will look at the key components of a good third wave teaching programme, and where products and software fit into it.

One of the other challenges experienced by teachers and by schools is that they often feel that they're held accountable to their ministries, to policymaking in education yet they don't feel they have an opportunity to implement the things that they would like to, to really make a difference.

There's an interesting piece of research that has come out regarding student performance and the factors which affect it.[8] Up to 59% of variance in student performance is attributable to differences between teachers and classes.

This means that a class teacher can make the most difference for a student. Regardless of government policies, ministry decisions, even school-based decisions, a class teacher has 59% of the ability to affect what goes on in that class.

And whilst 59% is up to the teacher, a further 21% is attributable to school-level variables. So, when we look at the school's capability to make change and the teacher's ability, a total of 80% of what can be done to make a difference comes from these two areas. For teachers, this is excellent information. Regardless of what goes on around us, it empowers us to make a difference in our classes and interactions with students.

I'd like to talk a little bit about how we view dyslexia. Traditionally, dyslexia has been viewed as a Specific Learning Disability. There is now a change of thinking with the advent of Functional Magnetic Resonance Imaging (FMRI),[9] so that we are now looking at dyslexia as more of a Specific Learning Difference, where the brain functions differently.

The past view is now considered to have been a major cause of underachievement amongst students and low expectations amongst teachers. The focus was on what was wrong with the student and focused on weaknesses rather than focusing on what was right and their strengths. The strengths model is now more often a preferred approach.[10]

If we speak to the last generation of people who have gone through school with dyslexia, many of them would tell us that they were put in the bottom classes at school. They felt stupid and have few good things to say about their educational experience.

To give you more understanding regarding what it is like to have dyslexia, and see those strengths and weaknesses, I would like to illustrate it through a scenario. This is an exercise that I often do in courses that I run with very interesting results.

I want you to close your eyes and I want you to imagine an orange tree in your mind, to picture it.

Usually, in any group, I have someone who gives me just a description of an orange tree. They're usually standing in front of the tree, and they'll describe some basic features of an orange tree. Usually things like shiny leaves, lots of oranges, often it's a small tree and they're standing in front of it.

Then I get somebody else, who interestingly sees an orange *tree,* rather than an *orange* tree! Their tree is coloured orange. And then I'll get people who describe a memory. It's a memory from their childhood, or an orange tree that they drive past each day.

I can remember asking this question of a dyslexic person, and I remember that it took quite a long time for him to give me an answer. When he finally answered the question, I got a very vivid description of an orange tree. He walked around the orange tree, he viewed it from every angle, he viewed it from above and he viewed it from below. It was a three-dimensional image that he described, and a very descriptive explanation came out.

One of the first things that struck me was he appeared to have a processing delay, and it took a long time to give me an answer. And yet when he gave his answer, it was so full and complete, I felt his answer was superior to the answers I often get to this question.

There is no doubt that people with dyslexia do have processing delays when it comes to completing language-based tasks, but one of the things that struck me in this situation was the length of time taken to get a response in relation to the quality of that response. Is it slow processing, or is it superior processing? It takes a lot longer to walk around a tree, look at it from every angle, seeing it three-dimensionally, and then to give a very vivid description, than it does to see a two-dimensional view and describe basic features. In education we have tended to see the weakness but not the strength.

Many of the last generation with learning difficulties went through school, disappointed with their experience there. They often left school thinking they were unintelligent. They often talk about enjoying sports and practical subjects, such as technology and home economics. We commonly hear the phrase, 'I went to school to eat my lunch.' As an adult, they often went into farming, and trades type careers. You often hear stories of people who are unable to pass trade exams or qualifications, but are still sought after due to their creative, and problem-solving abilities, and are often artistic and high achieving due to their three-dimensional thinking ability.

The common story depicted above is one that played out in our household. The world often says that the intelligent ones are the people who read and write well, and the people with degrees. I have two degrees, and am generally considered an intelligent person, but I really have to say that in many areas, I see that my husband's brain is superior to mine (I might regret the fact that I have ever said this in black and white). I think it's a tragedy that the world often values one type of intelligence over another, especially in education. There are so many other areas of intelligence, and the world would be a vastly poorer place if we had to do it without them. Many of the 'world's greats' – Einstein, Edison, Picasso, Dick Smith, Steve Jobs, Richard Branson, etc. – have made great contributions to the world. They think differently, and yet have spoken openly about their negative school experiences.

Because of this knowledge, and a change in thinking, we are working towards a change in education. Today's view is that we focus on the brain's preferences for learning. Whilst it recognises that there are some unexpected difficulties in the acquisition of certain skills, it also focuses on the strengths a person has. When we can make this change in education, then we're going to come through with a new generation of people with learning difficulties feeling very differently about themselves and their abilities.

I think there is a great deal of value in the British dyslexia-friendly schools' model, and Dyslexia Foundation's 4D model, and that these can go a long way to transforming and informing our practice in this area. I see an increasing understanding by schools that these changes are necessary. I see an increasing interest to develop policy and practice in third wave education to work towards that more inclusive model, which encourages and meets the needs of all at-risk learners. We owe it to at-risk groups with dyslexia, dyspraxia, those on the autism spectrum, children with Attention Deficit Hyperactivity Disorder (ADHD), and those with auditory and visual processing disorders, to provide equity in education, and give them positive experiences as they go through school.

One of the barriers to achieving this outcome is often hailed to be lack of funding.

Over the last few years, I've worked to develop and support an organisation called Education and Achievement Association, who have undergone a name change, from ADHD Rotorua to the present title. The name change is indicative of a change in thinking by parents and professionals, who are moving away from the 'deficit thinking' and the labels, and moving more towards raising achievement, improving outcomes and meeting needs.

In addition to the change in perception, there is a need to make the best use of limited funds. Funding in the past has come from philanthropic organisations and trusts. A lot of people are recognising, locally and internationally, that funding is becoming less and less available, and this is putting pressure on organisations who continue providing much needed services. The competition between not-for-profits and voluntary organisations, chasing elusive funding, is putting pressure on organisations to work together to collaborate and to achieve common goals. I see this as a huge opportunity for the various organisations that support individual groups in the learning difficulties/disabilities arena to make better use of funding by working together.

One of the problems that many schools have also identified is that there is little to no funding for third wave students. I have had several principals who have discussed rethinking their funding approach after attending a course I have run, and see the value in identifying first, second, third and fourth wave learners, and reviewing the funding resourcing and programmes they provide for each area. I believe this will be the attitude that is required as we move forward.

We are now increasingly recognising that we have offered third wave learners mainstream solutions, without achieving measurable outcomes. This is a waste of funds. Sadly, many third wave children have been through two, three or even four quality mainstream programmes with little benefit. Generally, this also severely affects self-esteem. I have had many children say to me, 'I am dumb,' and even, 'You can't teach me – lots of people have tried.'

In my experience, this is more a failure of the education system, than a failure of the students. With differentiated teaching, we can get a much better outcome.

What this is suggesting is that we need to identify our learner types, and then remediate in the most appropriate way. In New Zealand we have a lot of children who go onto Reading Recovery. Many of these children are third wave learners. The time on the programme doesn't help them, and unfortunately, they take the place of a second wave or mainstream child who would really benefit from the programme. We do know that the Reading Recovery programme can be a good solution for a mainstream student who is underachieving at age six, and needs time and strategies to improve reading achievement, but something else is needed which is more appropriate for a third wave child.

When we start to discuss the funding issue, it is all about using the funding we have in the best possible way. It is highly unlikely that more funding can be made available.

It's also about using teacher aides in the best possible way.[11] Currently, we often give our most needy students to the least trained people in our schools. I believe that teacher aides are a fantastic, but under-utilised resource. If we trained them well, they could be instrumental in raising achievement and improving outcomes.

It is very pleasing to see that not only have teacher aides been recognised in New Zealand recently, with a reasonably substantial pay increase, but also a pilot programme providing funds for teacher aide training has been made available.

A third area we can utilise funds more effectively, and raise achievement, is through the identification of vision and auditory problems. I mentioned earlier that when we were working with older students, many students had undiagnosed vision and hearing problems.

We now know that up to 70% of children with learning difficulties have some kind of visual problem, and most of these are not picked up by either the vision testing in schools or by optometrists. Behavioural optometrists specialise in learning and vision, and these children need to be seen by these professionals. I believe much of the remediation we are currently putting in is wasted because we have unaddressed vision issues. As a specialist teacher, I can employ all the best remediation skills I have, but the results will be limited if I have a child who has undiagnosed or unaddressed vision problems.

What I suggest is that schools put aside an amount of money, even a small amount of money, to help with identification. Working with behavioural optometrists, we have now developed training and resources for schools to address these problems in schools at low cost. Further discussion will follow on this later.

In summary, early identification is important for several reasons. When we identify students with difficulties early, they are much easier to remediate. It reduces the problems associated with learned helplessness, and the development of poor problem-solving strategies.

Early identification reduces negative impact on self-esteem. If students are allowed to continue on in education for a number of years with lack of success and feelings of underachievement, this becomes more and more difficult to address.

Finally, early identification reduces the cost of remediation. Children who are identified early require remediation for a shorter period of time than if we identify it at secondary school or beyond.

Early identification and teaching for diversity are optimal solutions for the issues facing education around at-risk learner groups. Achieving these fundamental changes will require equipping every teacher and school with the knowledge, skills and strategies to ensure they can identify and meet student needs at a classroom level. Without this we will continue to have 22% of the student population requiring the services of too few available specialists (RTLB/RTLit/Speech Language Therapists/Occupational Therapists, etc.).

We can't expect to follow the same path we always have and get a different outcome.

Chapter Five

What Is an Inclusive Model?

Already we can see that there are many benefits to developing a dyslexia-aware approach. Having a focus on at-risk student groups helps with early identification and cost-savings. We have talked about the benefits of a whole school approach to teacher development. A system where no student is left behind is a great philosophy to subscribe to, as we work towards this goal.

Sadly, the current situation is that our SLD students are over-represented in all the negative statistics.[1,2,3,4,5,6] As we have seen, these students make up many of the students who are stood down, suspended, or excluded. They utilise more social work and counselling services in schools. They have more drug and alcohol related issues. They are more likely to become involved with youth justice and the courts. They are over-represented in the suicide statistics and our jails.[1,2]

Many of the famous people who have learning differences have talked about two key things that made a positive difference for them. Firstly, that they found and work with their passions in life and secondly, they identify a person or people to support them with their areas of difficulty. I believe that our role as educators is to help those students who cross our paths to identify their strengths, and minimise their weaknesses, to assist them to move or stay away from the negative side of the ledger and move to the positive side of the ledger.

As educators, we are very aware of the importance that having quality relationships with our students plays in success and positive student outcomes. This relationship is even more important for students with dyslexia, ADHD, those on the spectrum, etc. Over the many years I have been working with these students and their schools, I have had some very interesting discussions on this topic.

Many children, from a young age, tell me they feel different, and they feel that often people, including teachers, don't understand them. I have been involved in many stand-down, suspension, and exclusion meetings. In my discussions with the students in a high school setting, they will very often say that out of the five or six teachers they work with, there are only one or two who like them and understand them. Interestingly, they often perform better in these classes. They often talk about one or two teachers who don't like them, and the other one or two teachers who they have neither positive or negative relationships with, and the students feel ambivalent towards them. Often these students do not get on well with authoritarian-type teachers who have fixed rules and ideas about how things should be. Our children often feel they get backed into a corner by these teachers, and their response is anger and frustration, which leads to 'an issue' that can result in the stand-down, suspension, or exclusion.

These children often have a strong sense of justice, they will fight battles that have nothing to do with them. They see things as black and white and often have difficulty putting themselves in someone else's shoes. All these characteristics have the potential to create problems and negative experiences that can result in these students being asked to leave school before they are ready.

Whilst this scenario is in a high school setting, I have often been told by parents that their children have only had one or two teachers in their entire school experience that really understood them, and as a result, they had a good year. When I raise this topic at parent meetings, parents reiterate the view that there are few teachers with the knowledge, understanding and skills necessary to support their children well.

The general feeling from parents is that it is the luck of the draw whether you get a good teacher or not and, in their words, going through school 'is like a lottery, and it shouldn't be this way.' The aim of this book, and my work, is to ensure that we change this experience in the education system, and that all teachers develop knowledge, understanding, the ability to differentiate their teaching, to teach for diversity and achieve quality outcomes for all students in a truly inclusive setting.

In New Zealand, we highly value an inclusive philosophy. Whilst I agree wholeheartedly with this philosophy, I feel we have some way to go before we can say that we have embraced this philosophy successfully.

In New Zealand, we are governed by the National Education Goals (NEGs),[7] and National Administration Guidelines (NAGs),[8] and we also have our Curriculum Document.[9] I had thought that because we weren't delivering equal education opportunities to all student groups, that this was something we hadn't considered or provided for in our system planning. But when I studied these documents, I was pleasantly surprised. In an earlier chapter, I discussed the NEGs and NAGs, but I re-state them here to accentuate this very important point.

In our NAGs,[8] it states that schools must develop and implement teaching and learning programmes:

a)

i) provide all students in years 1–10 with opportunities to progress and achieve for success in all areas of The National Curriculum;

ii) giving priority to student progress and achievement in literacy and numeracy and / or te reo matatini and pāngarau, especially in years 1–8;

b) through the analysis of good quality assessment information,* identify students and groups of students:

i) who are not progressing and / or achieving;

ii) who are at risk of not progressing and / or achieving;

iii) who have special needs (including gifted and talented students); and

iv) aspects of the curriculum which require special attention;

The NEGs state schools must provide:[7]

NEG 1

The highest standards of achievement, through programmes which enable students to realise their full potential as individuals …

NEG 2

Equality of educational opportunity for all New Zealanders, by identifying and removing barriers to achievement.

NEG 7

Success in their learning for those with special needs by ensuring that they are identified and receive appropriate support.

The New Zealand Curriculum Document states the requirements for boards of trustees.[9] I have included some pertinent extracts:

> Each board of trustees, through the principal and staff, is required to develop and implement a curriculum for students in years 1–13:
>
> - **that is underpinned by and consistent with the principles and values set out on page 9 [of the document];**
>
> Each board of trustees, through the principal and staff, is required to provide all students in years 1–10 with effectively taught programmes of learning in [all areas]:
>
> Each board of trustees, through the principal and staff, is required:
>
> - **to identify students and groups of students who are not achieving, who are at risk of not achieving, or who have special needs and to identify aspects of the curriculum that require particular attention;**

The document also discusses principles and values. One of these values is equity, which means that all students should have equal opportunity. One of the principles is inclusion, and there is a widespread belief that this only means classroom-based inclusion. To fulfil both requirements, students must be able to access the curriculum. If they are included, but can't learn, the equity value is not being met.

This is where I believe we are at today. Children are included, but they don't have equity and equal access to the curriculum. The mandate for change is already in our guiding documents, but currently we are not delivering as a sector what the document outlines. I further believe the reason we are not delivering what the document outlines is because we have trained our teachers, and the sector, in a mainstream teaching approach which doesn't cater for diversity or deliver differentiated teaching.

The question is, how do we create a truly inclusive model that walks the talk?

The current thinking is that we need to focus on the brain's preferences for learning, but we also need to recognise some unexpected difficulties in the acquisition of certain skills. If we also focus on the strengths an individual has, rather than the weaknesses, we have an environment that can bring about change.

In order or develop the truly inclusive model, we will need to make some adaptations to the mainstream teaching model to accommodate third wave needs.

The research in this area is still evolving but I believe there are seven key excellences for evidenced best practice, which provides the basis for effective third wave education.

The first of these is a multisensory approach. When the research first surfaced on learning styles, people were interested in finding out whether they were an auditory, visual, or kinaesthetic learner.[10] We now know that although people do have some kind of learning preferences, the current research asserts that people learn best when they have an opportunity to take in the learning through all the senses. This is true for everybody and as a result, a multisensory teaching approach needs to be evident in every classroom.

This has huge implications for teaching. In the past, schools have been recognised as providing predominantly auditory-learning environments. The people who have tended to do well at school are people who are good auditory learners and those who aren't, learn less well.[11,12,13,14,15,16] The new knowledge, that people learn best when they have an opportunity to take learning in through all the senses, is vital. As class teachers, this means we must adapt our teaching to cater for all the senses. One of the biggest changes I have had to make to my teaching is to learn how to plan and deliver more visual and kinaesthetic learning experiences. When preparing any lesson, unit or course, I now ask myself, *How does my planning cater for all modalities, rather than just working with my own preferred learning style, or sticking with the traditional auditory learning approach?*

As stated earlier, whilst multisensory teaching is important for everybody, it is even more important for people with auditory or visual processing problems. Most children with dyslexia have an auditory or visual weakness. Some children have both, which makes it even more difficult to remediate. There are also many children diagnosed with auditory and visual processing difficulties. If you've got an auditory weakness, then you're going to use your visual and kinaesthetic areas to fall back on, to develop your learning. If you have an auditory weakness and your class teacher works predominantly from an auditory modality, this places you further at risk. Conversely, if you've got a visual problem, you're going to be more reliant on auditory and kinaesthetic approaches. If you have a teacher who teaches predominantly through a visual modality, you will be more at risk. It is vital that teachers understand learning styles and adopt multisensory approaches if all students are to thrive.

The second strategy that is really important in a third wave classroom is having a very structured programme. Many people would probably say that schools are already structured places, and I would tend to agree, but what we often find is that it is not structured enough for children with Specific Learning Differences.

Children with SLD have personal organisational difficulties and so they rely on and need others to provide routine and structure. They don't cope well when those routines and structures are changed. How often do we have situations with these children on sports days, or class trips, when the normal class routines are interrupted? Think back to a situation where you were sick or required a reliever for the day because you were going to a course. Were there any students you worried about when you were not there? Chances are that it was all the third or fourth wave students. These students rely on their parents, their teachers, and their teacher aides to provide them with the structure they need to cope. If for some reason this isn't provided, their anxiety, frustration and anger can result in some very difficult situations.

The third key concept is that these children also need a very sequential learning system or learning approach, always focusing on the next steps in learning. This means that teachers will have to have a very good knowledge of the developmental stages of learning. They need to be able to assess and identify the stage a particular child is at, in all subject areas, and be working on the next step for that child in terms of their development. This is a huge challenge to a classroom teacher, as you may have 30 children who are at varying stages and have differing needs.

This is particularly challenging for secondary school teachers. Secondary school teachers have been trained in subject areas, and they're not trained in the developmental stages of learning. The expectation is that by the time children enter high school, they can read and write well enough to access the curriculum, and subject content is the focus. We are now finding that some children are entering high school at levels 2, 3 and 4 in curriculum achievement, not level 5 as required. Very often we are expecting teachers, who haven't had training in the developmental stages of learning, to support these students. Whilst many secondary schools are attempting to deal with this by employing some primary trained teachers, especially in the learning support area, we still largely have students going from class to class in a mainstream system, to teachers that do not have the training to assist them move forward step by step, from where they are now to where they need to be in the subject area.

One good example of a sequential learning programme is the Numeracy Project.[17] It has clearly identified learning stages, and there are key ideas which need to be mastered before a child moves on to the next stage. The numeracy booklets support class teachers through the developmental stages of learning, which advances children step by step to mastery of each level.

Another programme that I use, that is very structured and sequential in this area, is the Alpha to Omega integrated reading, writing, and spelling programme.[18] It looks at the developmental stages and provides an assessment for children around their letter–sound knowledge, their phonological awareness, and their knowledge of letter–sound patterns. The teaching begins from this point, and then works progressively through gaps in learning or developmental stages.

The challenge becomes, *How do you manage groups in a classroom where the students are at all different levels?* In New Zealand, in primary schools at least, we are taught in our training how to plan and teach in group settings. In Australia and in New Zealand secondary schools, whole class teaching is very often the focus. While whole class teaching works in a mainstream approach, it is largely unsuitable in a differentiated approach, where teaching for diversity needs to be the focus.

It is very common, at any year level, for there to be three or more different levels of children in the classroom. Unless we teach teachers how to differentiate and cater for different groups and needs, at-risk groups will remain. Grouping becomes very important, as does planning programmes to meet individual needs.

The fourth area that is essential for third wave learners is research-based, brain compatible teaching. The recent research in education and our ever-increasing knowledge of the brain is allowing us to establish better practices in education. One concept already discussed is multisensory teaching. Our knowledge of the latest research allows for better implementation and outcomes.

Being up to date with neuroscience and brain compatible learning enhances the uptake of learning. Another example is the recent information about the emotional centres of the brain.[19,20] We now know that the amygdala and the emotional centres of the brain are far more important in learning than we first thought. If children have physical needs that aren't met, such as adequate food and warm clothing, their learning ability will be affected. Children with emotional problems through home situations are more at risk. Children with learning difficulties experience high levels of anxiety, which further impacts their achievement levels. Knowing the detrimental effect of situations on the emotional centres on the brain, and their impact on learning, means we now need to address these problems if we are to meet individual need and raise student achievement.

Other research is showing the importance of short term and working memory in regard to learning, how memories are formed and how learning uptake can be increased.[21,22,23] This sort of information confirms the importance of adapting the way we teach in classrooms. We are also learning a lot about executive functioning, and how important this is.[24,25] Executive functioning refers to the set of skills and processes to do with managing self and resources, in order to achieve a goal. It is an umbrella term for the neurologically-based skills involving mental control and self-regulation. Children with good executive functioning skills have greater success in learning. At-risk students are recognised as having poorer executive functioning skills. The explicit teaching of executive functioning skills is now becoming increasingly recognised as being important to raise achievement for these students.

The fifth metaphorical key change that is required relates to repetition and overlearning.[26,27]

It is believed that if the average child takes 7 times to learn something, children with learning difficulties can take up to 49 times to consolidate learning.[28] This has huge implications for the classroom teacher. How do you maintain and extend learning for the quick learners, while you are providing repetition and overlearning for others? How do you support the needs of at-risk learners, while you are working with mainstream and advanced learners? Whilst teachers do have and use strategies to address a variety of student needs, I believe we haven't gone anywhere near the amount of repetition and overlearning that is required for third wave students. One reason is that we haven't understood this concept fully. Another reason is it is virtually impossible for a class teacher to organise this, in a classroom setting, without help.

To address this, what I recommend is a team approach:

- **Class teachers to focus on teaching 7 times, using best practice teaching that meets the needs of students.**
- **Specialist teachers – RTLB/RTLit/SENCO/ SPELD or other specialists – to deliver one or two sessions a week. It is unlikely, due to cost, that they will be able to deliver more than one or two sessions per week.**
- **Well trained teacher aides to provide repetition and overlearning third wave programmes for three sessions a week, with targeted, identified students.**
- **Parents to support child and offer home learning.**
- **Appropriate software and computer programmes to be used.**

Being a teacher, and a parent of a child with a learning difficulty, I have good understanding of the challenges faced by schools. I believe as a parent of a child who requires more support, that I have an obligation to support the school, and my child.

Most parents do not have the understanding or the skills, so I believe it is important that we run parent sessions to provide them with information and training. Many families can provide parent, grandparent, or other family member support, and we encourage three sessions a week once the school has trained the family member. For children who, for one reason or another, are not able to have the benefit of home support, trained community volunteers can be used. Volunteers can come from church groups or senior citizens groups, and places like Lions Groups and Rotary are often great sources of adult tutors.

The use of software is another great way to ensure sufficient repetition and overlearning. Programmes such as Maths Buddy,[29] Mathletics,[30] Literacy Planet,[31] STEPS Learning Staircase,[32] Jungle Memory,[33] Lumosity,[34] and Word Chain[35] are excellent tools to support students further.

Through this process we have moved from a situation where we have a class teacher that is largely solely responsible and unable to provide fully for what is needed, to a situation where the class teacher is responsible for organising and managing the approach, but the delivery is implemented through several initiatives.

The sixth concept that is really important is diagnostic evidence. Our assessment needs to be robust. We do need to know the weaknesses and the strengths each child has. Knowing strengths allows us to use these to support teaching, and knowing weaknesses, or next steps, provides the basis of our planning and teaching. We will be looking at specialist assessment in a later chapter but for now we need to consider what the information is telling us, and how we can use this information diagnostically to support the child further.

The seventh idea I would like to discuss is the explicit teaching of metacognitive strategies. I have had this understanding brought home to me personally, in my own education, and the experience that I had was profound.

I started school in England at the age of 4. When I was 10, we came out to New Zealand. As you will appreciate, the school years are different, and they had to decide how they would place our family of five children: six months ahead or six months behind. They gave us all an IQ test and decided that we should be placed in the year above.

Now, because I started school at 4 years, I was 18 months younger than most of the students in my class. I remember going through intermediate and high school, and absolutely struggling. I used to work very hard. I remember studying three hours a night, always studying for tests, always doing homework, and studying for exams. I was a really diligent student.

For all my efforts, I failed School C. I remember, to this day, that I got 50 for Geography, 51 for English, 43 for Science, 42 for Maths and 40 for French. After all that work, the disappointment that I felt was huge. They did let me go on into the sixth form, and I ended up getting 30% for all the mid-year exams. I started wagging school, and then I dropped out.

I went out to the workforce, and 18 months later I came back to school as an adult student. I worked hard, and with the extra maturity, I finished my sixth form year and I got accredited. I applied and went off to teachers' college. I remember going through teachers' college, feeling really concerned that I was going to fail everything. I ended up being a C+ student, and I got the odd B.

At the age of 40, I decided to go back to university to complete my degree. I had six papers to do over the year, and I was teaching at the same time. I started at summer school, and I did a paper called Sociology. I can remember joking that I didn't even know what sociology was.

The first unit of work on the agenda was 'learning to learn.' We talked about learning strategies, and how effective learners learn best. I remember feeling a sense of being overwhelmed.

The lecturer said that effective learners read the material and relate the material to their own personal experience. She said that good learners don't read things over and over, and they don't learn things off by heart. They use mind maps, they look at key words, they use colour, because the brain remembers colours. She talked about all of these effective learning strategies that I had never used.

I can remember thinking, *If this lady knows what she is talking about, then I am 40 years of age, I have been a teacher for quite some time, and I know nothing about learning.*

I remember thinking she must be wrong. A couple of days later, she announced a test and I decided I was going to prove that she was wrong. I decided I was going to throw out everything I knew about learning, and I was just going to do exactly what she said. I didn't overstudy, I didn't learn anything off by heart, I didn't read things repeatedly. I related the material to what I knew, I didn't study late, and I didn't get up the morning of the test and do further study. I did some mind maps in colour, and looked at key words, and then I just went into the test and did my best.

The test seemed to go pretty well. I remember that there were about 200 people doing the summer school paper.

At university, when I was there, the usual system was that when the exam or test results came out, everybody had a student ID number, and they would put the marks on the wall next to the student ID numbers. You could go up find your ID number and get your mark.

I went up to the board and I looked up my student ID and there was a 1 beside my number. I thought, *Oh I've made a mistake, it can't be the right number.* I went to my bag, got my student ID card, and I one-to-one matched the numbers. I realised that I had come first out of 200 people!

I thought, *Oh my goodness, that actually does mean that I'm 40 years of age, I've been a teacher for all this time and I really haven't known a lot about learning. This is a problem.*

This was an absolutely life changing moment for me.

I went on to complete that paper, and we had a final exam. I came equal second in that exam. Basically, since then, I have become an A student.

I am really thankful now for having had that experience, because I now know that I'm a third wave learner. I have many of the traits of inattentive type ADHD. I know first-hand that third wave learners don't pick up metacognitive strategies without being taught. These need to be specifically taught and practised.

As if to reiterate these points, I had another experience in one of the seminars I ran. I had a secondary school teacher tell me that she marks NCEA exam papers. She said, 'Every year I get given a stack of exam papers, and I flip through them and put them in two piles. I look for evidence that anyone has used strategies – planning, mind maps, highlighted key words, planned use of time, etc. I put those papers in one pile. In the other pile go all the papers where there is no evidence of planning strategies. Every year, without fail, the pile that uses strategies are the highest achieving, and those who don't are the lowest.'

This is vital information for teachers. Although one might think we've talked a lot about metacognitive strategies over the last few years, and that we teach them, I don't think we have taught them as explicitly as is necessary and given the opportunities for repetition and overlearning at the level needed for third wave learners.

In teaching metacognitive strategies, we need to work out which strategy to use, when to use it, how to use it, and why are we using it. First wave children work this out without being taught. They often figure out the quickest and the best ways of doing things and will even tell you. Second wave learners need to be taught metacognitive strategies and given an opportunity to use them throughout their learning. If third wave learners don't get specific explicit metacognitive strategy teaching, and many chances for practise, they don't learn strategies for success.

In addition to these seven key excellences, I believe there is one more change we need to make and that is to focus on underpinning cognitive weaknesses. If we have a child who has visual problems and we don't address those visual problems, they will struggle to go on to academic learning and achievement. If a child has got scanning and tracking problems, we need to address this and give visual training before they can read well enough to succeed. We can give reading, reading, reading and more reading, but if we don't address visual problems first, the progress students make is much slower.

We know that short term and working memory is important for learning. To improve short term and working memory, as part of the programme to raise achievement, makes sense.

We know that good executive functioning and decision-making ability is required for achievement, and at-risk students often have difficulties in these areas. Teaching skills and strategies, and providing practise, makes sense if we want to raise achievement and improve outcomes. These are just a few examples of the many underpinning cognitive weaknesses that need addressing.

In this chapter, we have discussed inclusiveness and what it means. We have looked at the expectations for schools in the NEGs, NAGs, and the New Zealand Curriculum Document, in relation to at-risk learner groups. We have begun to look at the seven key excellences, and adaptations to teaching that will be needed, to effect change for our underachieving groups. The key point is that when we make these changes, all learner groups will benefit.

We are working toward a more focused approach that offers multisensory teaching, and a structured programme that is sequential in nature. The programme needs to utilise researched best practice and include repetition and overlearning. In addition, it must be based on diagnostic evidence, focus on metacognitive strategies, and address underpinning cognitive weaknesses. This approach gives each child the best chance of reaching their potential.

Chapter Six

Traditional vs. Modern Approaches

In 2013, I was lucky enough to attend the Australian Council for Educational Research (ACER) Conference in Melbourne. One of the guest speakers – Martin Westwell, a strategic professor in the science of learning from Flinders University – spoke about when education and neuroscience meet the Australian curriculum.[1]

His talk resonated with me. He talked about needing to move from an industrial model to a post-industrial model of education. The industrial – the common, mainstream approach – has been a very linear and hierarchical system. A lot of our curriculum is content based. It wasn't so long ago that we had pass rates, and only a certain number of students were allowed to pass, and we used to scale up or scale down marks, depending on the percentages. The system requires student compliance, and we expect students to jump through various hoops as they go through the system.

We're now recognising that change from this approach is needed. We need to be more concerned about what is effective learning. It's not what we teach that matters; it's what the students learn. Our teaching needs to be more strategic in its intent, where the higher order thinking skills such as problem solving, reasoning, and making inferences and judgements are more of the focus. Although some change has occurred, and we have moved towards a more post-industrial methodology, we are really not there yet.

Westwell talked about the need to teach three skills. Firstly, he talked about the need to stop and think. To help children take control of their actions and thoughts, to manage impulse inhibition.

The second key concept he discussed was regarding teaching working memory. We know through research that working memory is a prerequisite to successful learning.[1,2,3]

Thirdly, he talked about cognitive flexibility – the ability to switch gears, and to adjust to changing demands. Cognitive flexibility is the ability to prioritise and look at things from different perspectives. One thing that struck me about Westwell's talk was that he was talking about general education and mainstream approaches, and I realised as he was saying this that our at-risk learners need these things even more. The very things he discusses are often part of the underpinning cognitive weaknesses that we identify with children who are diagnosed with various learning difficulties and differences.

When young people are expected to interpret and infer, it puts an enormous demand on executive functions. The extent to which young people have developed executive functions has been shown to profoundly affect their outcomes, in terms of education, health, income and criminal behaviour.

Westwell cited the New Zealand Dunedin study,[3] where they followed a thousand children from birth to adulthood, and they found that children with lower levels of self-control are more likely to leave school without formal qualifications. They're more likely to have a criminal conviction. They're more likely to have financial difficulties, a lower income, and a lower socio-economic status. They will also have poorer health outcomes by the age of 32 years old.

These are significant findings. If these needs and problems are not addressed, we are consigning children to lead poor quality lives, as a result of poor decision making and poor self-control. This leads to lower qualifications, lower income, etc. In education, we have a professional and moral responsibility to identify these learners and address these issues.

Westwell went on to explain that typically children from a low socio-economic status have lower levels of self-control and executive functions, and resultingly less cognitive capacity to support their day-to-day decision-making processes. In turn, this prevents them from engaging with educational opportunities, and attracts them into lower income, lower socio-economic circumstances, and poorer health outcomes.

Also, as poverty and lower socio-economic status does run in families, people might be tempted to think that this is genetic. Whilst it is likely that there's a genetic component, the characteristics of the environment have been shown to be crucially important.

Largely, children are not genetically pre-destined to be at-risk learners. Children who are well supported will develop executive functions and enjoy much better outcomes than those who do not.[4] The Dunedin study suggests that the level of executive function can be improved in individuals who are supported, which is really exciting news for us as educators. Enhanced skills will lead to better outcomes, including higher educational attainment, better socio-economic status, etc.

Westwell concluded that the industrial model of education no longer serves the needs of any of our young people, to be effective children and adolescents in the modern world, or to prepare them for an uncertain future. With these findings in mind, we need to prepare our children for this uncertain future. Moving from an industrial educational philosophy to a post-industrial system of teaching is critical.

Barbara Arrowsmith also spoke at the ACER Conference.[5] She is the Canadian educator who is known as 'the woman who changed her brain.'

Arrowsmith talked about the advances in neuroscience, and how through Magnetic Resonance Imaging (MRI), we can now identify which areas of the brain and networks are involved in behaviour and learning. This can also tell us about abnormal development, and which regions are not functioning normally, and indicate those that could benefit from intervention. We can create cognitive programmes to stimulate and strengthen the functioning of these areas using neuroplasticity.

The term 'neuroplasticity' refers to the brain's ability to change, structurally and functionally, in response to stimulation. It can grow dendrites (the part of a neuron that receives signals to activate the neuron) and make new neural connections. This changes the brain's capacity to learn and to function. This is a very exciting breakthrough, educationally, because this means we can develop and strengthen weak areas of the brain and make change. Something we need to take into consideration is that these changes can be positive or negative. We need to understand how we can effectively reduce factors leading to negative neural changes, and how can we increase factors that lead to positive changes.

Negative changes can occur if people are exposed to chronic negative stress or prolonged anxiety. We are seeing increasing numbers of students diagnosed with anxiety disorders. Teachers have commented that the stress levels in students is on the increase. There is a school of thought that the changes in assessment policies have created new problems. Previously, when exams were largely at midyear and the end of the year, student stress peaked at these times and then diminished in between. Now that we have assessment right throughout the year, we are seeing heightened stress levels continuously. We have already discussed how stress and anxiety impacts achievement. Many students with learning difficulties, and those on the autism spectrum, have additional anxiety as a result of the problems connected to learning difficulties and the frustration that goes with it. Social problems, including not fitting in or being understood by others, can add to this. All these issues result in negative brain changes.

Knowing what causes positive brain changes is vitally important. Firstly, we know that active, sustained engagement facilitates these positive changes. We know student engagement is important in education, but the key words here are 'active' and 'sustained.' Using a problem-solving approach sets up active engagement, and when students are interested in the learning topic or idea, sustaining attention requires less effort.

Environmental enrichment also creates positive brain changes. Setting up an environment, both emotionally and physically, that is conducive to learning is an additional prerequisite.

Task demand must also be considered. It's very important that teachers know what stage a student is at now and have them working just above that level. If the task is too difficult, they've got nothing to connect knowledge and information to. If it's too easy, then they're not being asked to extend themselves.

Effortful processing is also believed to create positive brain changes. This means processing ideas and metacognitive strategies in an effortful way. Brain compatible learning has taught us that novelty and complexity increases learning.[6] A colleague of mine – Mike Scaddan, a specialist in neurosciences and brain compatible learning – often reminds me of this point. Mike has these amazing hats, and whenever he is about to say something vitally important, he selects a novelty hat and makes the statement. A person remembers and links the statement to the hat. It is very much like choosing the right bottle of wine for a meal. He has the right hat for the purpose.

We also know that exercise is important for learning. It often worries me when we take children out of classes like physical education, which they often like and need, to give them additional literacy or specialist lessons. Perhaps this practice is not conducive to those positive brain changes that we're looking for.

Rewards are another way of enhancing positive brain changes.[7] There has been some very interesting research around rewards recently. This research shows it is not so much the reward itself, but it's the chance of the reward that spurs children on positively. In a recent study, they gave children the opportunity of choosing an immediate reward for answering one question right, or waiting until they got three questions right, and they would double the reward. There was a spike in dopamine that occurred at the chance of a reward. A lot of children would go for the delayed reward, and the chance of getting more.

Another thing that causes positive brain changes is a performance feedback system. The way that we actually feed information back to children is important. Third wave learners need a lot more formal feedback.[8] It is important that they receive both verbal and written feedback which is specific in relation to the skills and strategies that they're using well. Effective feedback causes positive brain changes.

Having knowledge about the ways in which the brain can be positively affected allows us to set up conditions in the classroom to maximise benefits and create situations to ensure this is achieved. Conversely, knowing these negative effects on the brain allows us to address the situations we are aware of, and avoid creating negative effects as much as possible.

Arrowsmith also talked about how the brains of dyslexic people function differently.[5] She talked about intensive remediation targeting phonological or auditory processing. Children with dyslexia show increased brain activity in multiple brain areas after remediation. We can now see differences in brain function through MRI scans, pre- and post-intervention.

In her ACER Conference presentation, Arrowsmith reiterated that working memory capacity has been found to be a strong predictor of future academic success. Several studies show that working memory training leads to activation changes in the frontal-parietal network, which leads to improved performance on tasks requiring working memory, and those involving intentional control.

Much of what Arrowsmith talked about, I understood from my training with SPELD in New Zealand. Much of the current research is verifying the premises which SPELD built its foundations on over 30 years ago,[9,10] when the technology to back up their methodology was not available. This research is now paving the way for changes to be made in teaching and classroom practice.

Whilst this reference to Arrowsmith is not intended to be a review of the effectiveness of her programme, the research information she cited in her talk is very relevant to this discussion.

As a result of research into working memory, Auckland University has been developing a working memory training programme that will be available to all schools in the near future, the MovinCog Programme.[11] Their research has shown that working memory training is enhanced further when it is accompanied by physical activity, probably due to activating kinaesthetic modalities along with visual and/or auditory. The programme will include 10–15 minutes physical activity alongside the working memory training.

An example of where we might measure the outcomes of such a programme is in numeracy. Many students who have learning difficulties struggle with number concepts. In maths, you need to hold and manipulate numbers in your head to solve problems. Children with poor maths abilities are often shown to have poor working memory and processing delays. We could continue to address problems mathematically by giving more maths work, with a different programme or a different person. However, by addressing the underpinning cognitive weakness through working memory training, we would be addressing the root cause of the problem.

Arrowsmith concludes that rather than change the way we teach, what is needed is to include cognitive programmes as part of the curriculum. Students would actually spend part of their day training their brain.

Whilst the traditional view has focused on weaknesses, the modern proposed view encourages us to focus on strengths. Often people with learning differences are highly imaginative. They're creative. These children are often natural thinkers, who develop original solutions to problems.

They have an ability to think in pictures, sometimes with a strong artistic talent, and often have a strong visual preference for information acquisition. Many of these students are socially and verbally able; they may enjoy drama and sport; they typically demonstrate ability in science and in maths. They enjoy technology or current affairs, and they often have a really good general knowledge to match. Specific differences produce specific benefits. For example, dyslexia often enables learners to be curious and eclectic, and find the creative links and patterns that can be unclear to others.

I am often surprised by some of the discussions you have with these children. For example, a lengthy conversation regarding the floating plastic bubble of rubbish that's in the sea. One person once spoke to me for almost an hour about the world's water shortage. She discussed things that I hadn't even considered before.

Often when we're talking with children on the mat or in class discussions, they seem to say something off topic or irrelevant. On occasion I have taken the time pursue a child's comment and find they have seen an obscure link between what we are talking about and what is in their head. Very often, they are several steps ahead of our conversation, but it appears at the time that they're off task.

Often, people with dyslexia and learning difficulties are average to above average in intelligence. 10–15% of children with learning differences will also be gifted. They're good problem solvers, they're also very passionate about areas of interest and they usually have one or two passionate hobbies that they are very good at or know a lot about. They're often interested in nature and animals. They're frequently good at performing arts, visual arts, and music.

These children do, however, have unexpected problems in literacy, and often numeracy. They do require special ways of teaching to minimise the problems, and to maximise their potential.

To date, schools have tended to focus on their weaknesses, but not so much on their strengths. Because so much about school is about reading and writing, it highlights all the areas that are problematic for those with learning difficulties such as dyslexia. This has had a huge negative impact on self-esteem for these students.

These children are very vulnerable as learners, if reading and spelling are allowed to detract from information processing. Their core thinking skills and their knowledge is as good as their peers, if not better. It is the reading and writing that's the problem.

In summary, we can see that the traditional approaches haven't supported those with learning differences well. It is imperative that we move to a modern approach which focuses on differentiated teaching, incorporating the features of quality education, as is highlighted through neuroscience and modern research. This will place the focus on the students' strengths, which will support and preserve a positive self-esteem, but at the same time focus on weak areas. This approach emphasises the importance of teaching the child in the way that they learn best and allowing them to maximise achievement and reach potential in academic learning.

Chapter Seven

What Does an Inclusive Classroom Look Like?

Dyslexia and other learning difficulties can be mild, moderate, or extremely challenging. We can think of this as a continuum, where some people are mildly affected and others more significantly. Despite this, our 22% figures from our model means we are looking at significant numbers.[1,2,3,4,5,6,7]

We do know that for children with learning differences, there is a strong hereditary component.[8] From MRI scans, we know that there is a neurological difference in brain function.[9,10] It's widely recognised that those with learning differences do have a different way of thinking.

This is often a picture-based, three-dimensional type thinking, and we recognise it is a lifetime experience. Whilst in the past, our thinking may have been that it is a condition we need to cure, many now recognise that it is almost insulting to talk about cures. When we say we want to cure something, it implies that something is wrong. However, when we look at the benefits that are associated with learning difficulties and differences, these things are also something to be valued.

These people have great strengths,[11] but they do have unexpected weaknesses. There are creative opportunities, but there are also behavioural challenges around people with learning differences. Part of the behavioural challenge is due to the frustration and anxiety that our school system creates, or exacerbates, because very often it doesn't understand or meet the needs of students who learn differently.

A philosophy adopted by the Dyslexia Foundation 4D approach from Neil Mackay is very useful as a starting point.[12] 'Notice and Adjust' allows us to observe and identify differences and make adjustments for preferences. We want to ensure that differentiation is inherent in mainstream practice. We want to focus on strengths, not just weaknesses.

In chapter five, I discussed the idea that because our education system wasn't catering for children who learn differently, that maybe the system wasn't geared up to cater for these children. I shared that I had realised to my surprise, there is a lot already contained within the Curriculum Document. As a result of this, our goal needs to be implementation of the spirit, ethos, and philosophy of the National Curriculum, rather than to create a philosophy to embed in our guiding documents.

I would like to look further into the document now, and see how it supports schools, teachers and students who learn differently. Our national vision, as outlined in the New Zealand Curriculum document,[13] says that we want young people who will be confident, connected, actively involved and lifelong learners. I am sure you will agree that this is something great to aspire to and is something that we want for all our children.

Other values highlighted in the Curriculum Document are:

- **Excellence**
- **Innovation**
- **Inquiry and curiosity**
- **Diversity**

- **Ecological sustainability**
- **Integrity**
- **Respect**
- **Equity.**

The Curriculum Document also talks about the following principles:

- **Inclusion**
- **Learning to learn**
- **Community engagement**
- **Coherence**
- **A future focus**
- **High expectations**
- **Cultural diversity.**

When I consider all my teaching experience, from working in Bay of Plenty schools to running seminars across New Zealand, and undertaking whole school professional development nationally, I can hold my hand on my heart and say we do the best we can to deliver the majority of these expectations, to the majority of students. I can't, however, honestly say that we deliver these values and expectations to the at-risk groups in education. I can't say that these students have equal opportunity, or that they are able to access the curriculum and achieve outcomes that match their potential. If we were able to do a calculation of the number of children in education in New Zealand schools, and consider 22% of them, we would have a very big number. This number of students underachieving, utilising specialist assistance and support services, and making up a large number of society's negative statistics, is a huge drain on society. In addition, and equally important, is the individual cost to a young person of not being able to achieve their potential, and possibly not making the valid contribution to society that they are able to. The problems associated with this also affect their families and networks.

Whilst we may be able to say that we support the majority well in education, we can hardly say that remaining number are a small minority. This book is dedicated to exploring, discussing, evaluating, and remediating the inequities in education, so that we can include the at-risk student groups in the values we have in education. It is important to acknowledge that as a profession, we have underachieved in this area. As a sector, it is now time to embrace and commit to change, to realise positive outcomes for students who have, until now, been marginalised.

Along with this vision, and these principles and values, we want to develop the key competencies for all students enrolled in education. We want to support the development of thinking, using language symbols in texts, self-management, the ability to relate to others and to participate and contribute.

To do this, we can look again to the NEGs and the NAGs and expand on what we talked about earlier. NEG 7 talks about success and learning for those with special needs,[14] ensuring they are identified and receive appropriate support. I think if you talk to schools, if you talk to teachers and indeed if you talk to parents, most would concur that we're not achieving this, and that we don't have the resources currently to give the appropriate support to students who fit the third wave criteria.

The next questions we need to ask are, what does all this mean to schools, and what does this mean for us as teachers? I have often said that I don't believe the cavalry is coming. I do not believe that funding, guidelines, resources, and solutions are going to be provided for us. I think there are few people in decision-making places who truly understand this problem and have policies and practice to address it.

If there were, we wouldn't still have a long tail of underachievers in education, and we wouldn't have a problem of this magnitude. However, what I do believe is that the solution to this problem belongs to the sector. I believe that we already have the knowledge, the power, and the ability to effect change, and make measurable, positive differences to individuals and at-risk groups that are part of this challenge. Our job is now to mobilise our knowledge and resources, and lead change in education, with the knowledge we already have.

Our first step needs to be to create the environment. We want to be able to minimise the fear of disapproval, the lack of understanding, that has surrounded people with learning differences in the past. We also want to minimise the fear of failure. When you speak to many students who have gone through the education system, they talk about fear of failure, and trying to hide the fact that they had learning difficulties.

We also want to minimise the fear of tests by giving assessment choices. Because exams and tests focus on reading and writing, which are frequently weak areas for those with learning differences, it puts these learners at a disadvantage. We are testing people on their weaknesses, rather than testing people on their strengths. To address this, we need to give assessment choices and differentiated assessment.

We also want to minimise the fear of reading out loud. Gone are the days when we required students to read out loud in groups or class settings, and we can look at other reading strategies that support students much better.

As a teacher, we also want to find out about the student's strengths, so that we can use their strengths to support their weaknesses. We want to be able to notice and identify things about children and make adjustments in the way that we're teaching. We want to create a much more personalised learning approach, where instead of one size fits all, we look at the needs of the child and then create our programme around that.

Our work can now be much more research based,[15,16] where we are able to explain our practice, and why we are doing the things that we are doing. Our philosophies and our practice are based on brain-compatible learning. I have had an increasing concern that many of the best practice strategies that are being espoused are strategies suited to mainstream learners. What is good for a mainstream learner, is not necessarily good for a third wave learner, and unfortunately, we have been quoted best practice like it is.

An example of this is the development of innovative learning environment/spaces. There has been a lot of research regarding the effectiveness of this teaching model,[17] hence the reason why we are implementing them. Unfortunately, if you are a third wave learner with auditory and visual processing difficulties, innovative learning environments can make it even more difficult for you to learn. Students with distractibility, and visual and auditory figure-ground challenges, are more likely to be at risk in these learning environments. Through proper understanding, and teacher training in the use of innovative learning environments, the negative effects can be lessened. Unfortunately, this has not been addressed across the sector effectively and we have teachers and students saying that third wave learners' achievement is being negatively affected.[18]

I am not saying that we shouldn't have innovative learning environments. What I am saying is, just as we value differentiated teaching, we need to value differentiated learning environments. Schools need to have alternatives and strategies in place to cater for those students for whom modern learning environments are not the optimal solution. It is simply not okay to say the research says that modern learning environments are a best practice approach and overlook the needs of students for whom it is not best practice.

With neuroscience and brain-compatible learning concepts, we are beginning to have more research on what is and isn't best practice for third wave students. It is fair to say that we don't have a comparable body of evidence for best practice third wave education, to what we have for mainstream education. We have been applying mainstream philosophy to third wave students, without success, for many years. This can be evidenced by the number of students who have been through remediation programmes, such as Reading Recovery, Rainbow Reading, PPP, etc. They have also worked with RTLB, RTLit, worked with SENCOs, had extra teacher aide time, and are still performing well below their chronological age. In many cases, they are still three or more years below their chronological age in achievement. As a sector, we now need to accept that what we have been doing isn't working for these students, and we need to look at modern research, and create more of it, to find solutions to the third wave education problem.

We want to set this group up for success. In the past, I think many students with learning differences would say that they'd been set up to fail. We want to focus on what they're doing right, and we want to recognise and acknowledge strengths.

Multisensory teaching is a key concept that we need to make universal best practice.

Many of us grew up in a predominantly auditory teaching environment.

For many teachers, and I would include myself as one of these, left to our own devices, we are probably good auditory teachers. For me, it's been a real challenge to develop my teaching so that I am recognising other learning preferences.

Visual Learning Strategies

Learning to keep it visual has been something of a challenge. To make classrooms and classes more visual places, we can use and teach mind mapping and brainstorming techniques. Tony Buzan brought out a lot of these techniques.[19] Brain-compatible learning showed us that the brain remembers and stores information better when colour is used. We can incorporate this into our teaching. Using few words to portray ideas, and using pictures and mind maps, are things we can do to enhance the brain's capacity to remember and to learn.

A great visual representation by a colleague.[21]

Strategies to keep learning visual:

- **Mind maps**
- **Visual timetables**
- **Using and teaching the use of highlighters – the Key Comprehension Resource is a great tool for teaching this**[20]
- **Teaching key words**
- **Labelling resources**
- **Use of diagrams.**

Today we recognise the value of highlighters, but I don't ever remember being taught how to use them. We do teach key words. Many students, when asked to highlight key words, highlight everything. Explicitly teaching key words, and the use of highlighters, keeps learning more visual. Whilst the first and second wave learners may pick this up more easily, our third wave learners need explicit teaching and practise with all these skills and strategies.

One of the difficulties we see children display, when we do specialist assessments, is that they often have trouble with rapid naming. It's almost like the filing system in the brain can't find the right words quickly. A simple strategy like labelling resources in the classroom improves rapid naming ability. We will often do this for teaching a second language, but we wouldn't necessarily do it for a primary language. Labelling resources helps children practise rapid retrieval.

Using diagrams for learning to expand on auditory explanations can be very valuable, also. An example of this would be if we have a young person who has difficulty with writing, and we want them to write a paragraph to explain their knowledge of something in science, this could be a challenge that results in underachievement. It would be equally valid for them to draw us a diagram, label it, and use some key words to explain functions. This means a student isn't being asked to show their knowledge in a way that makes them use their weaker skill.

Tools like visual timetables assist children who get confused about where they should be, when they need to be there, and what gear they need at the time. It may be difficult for people without learning difficulties to understand why this is necessary, but for many at-risk learners this can be an extreme challenge.

For example, every year, a few children miss their exams because they got the wrong day, or they went in the afternoon when it was a morning exam. It is hard for people who don't have a learning difficulty to comprehend how somebody could make such a mistake, but for third wave learners, organisation and getting confused can be a big problem.

I remember having a young student who was going from intermediate to secondary school, and he was doing a new school orientation session. After the first term in his new school, he was getting into trouble a lot. He was late to class, and he never had the right gear that he needed. I remember him saying, 'I don't know how to use the locker system.' People had explained it to him several times, but what that student needed was to be shown. He needed someone to take him to the locker, first thing in the morning, and say, 'Let's look at your timetable, these are the classes that you've got in periods one or two, and so you need these books. Then we're going to come back here at morning teatime; you're going to put these books away and you're going to take the books that you need for the next classes out. You will do the same again at lunchtime,' and so on.

He needed to see it, and do it before he understood it. He couldn't process the information when someone explained it auditorily. Again, it is hard for teachers and others who don't have a learning difficulty to understand, but this young man ended up having behaviour problems. He was getting in trouble regularly. He was suspended, he was getting detentions. Largely, it was due to an unaddressed learning problem. If we can sort out the underlying reason(s) and address it/them, the problems often go away.

Other Strategies to Support Third Wave Learners

As well as developing a multisensory programme, more explicit, step-by-step structured teaching is required, including careful monitoring of a child's learning. Often this requires more written and verbal feedback. This can be challenging to class teachers. With up to 30 students in a class, time is limited. I suggest that each class teacher identify the five or six third wave learners in their class, and ensure more regular, specific, and comprehensive feedback is given in a verbal and written form for those students. The feedback should focus on the skills and strategies being taught and provide key information about what they are doing well, and what they need to focus on next.

Chances are, the level and type of feedback currently being given is sufficient for first and second wave students. In addition, these students may be capable of some self-monitoring. In many cases, first wave students will be able to tell you the best or quicker ways of doing something. If asked what did you do well, and what would you want to improve on next time, they could probably tell you quite accurately. Setting up a buddy or peer review programme with first and second wave learners could also assist with this process. Basically, what you want to achieve here is a reduced time input into the feedback process, by giving each student group what they need. In essence, we are differentiating our feedback systems based on student need.

We also need to look at setting up a partnership between child, family, and school, so that we can get home involved with the repetition and overlearning process. Ideally, I recommend that this is done on a school-wide basis and set up by the SENCO. Tutor reading, writing, spelling, a junior school language programme and even numeracy programmes can facilitate this process. If, for some reason, this is not picked up as a whole school approach, I recommend class teachers determine the class needs and priorities and establish this for their own class. We will discuss how this can be done in later chapters.

We also want clear intentions and success criteria. We have got a lot better in this area over recent years. I can remember in my generation, the idea of objectives, and what we were meant to learn, was never discussed. These days, objectives are usually written up on the board in high schools. In primary school we have 'WALTs', or 'We Are Learning To …' and 'WILFs', or 'What I'm Looking For'. This makes it so much easier for the children to grasp what they're meant to be learning. The only thing I would add here is that for third wave learners, we need to make this explicit. We may need to check that the student knows, and can explain, what the objective is. We can't assume that having it on the board, or discussing it at the beginning of a lesson, is enough.

To enhance achievement, we will want to:

- **Make the best use of strengths, and learning preferences**

- **Ensure that our classes are very structured**

- **Provide step-by-step instructions, and take one step at a time**

- **Encourage and praise questions. Many of our children have difficulty formulating questions, as they don't know how to ask about what they don't know. We may have to encourage and teach children how to ask questions.**

We often talk about a philosophy in third wave education that 'less is often more.' Many times, the pace in a mainstream class doesn't allow a third wave student to keep up. They can often go from lesson to lesson not achieving anything, because either the pace is too quick, or the material is over their head. By slowing things down and ensuring that children are working on their next steps, we can reverse the individual experience of non-achievement. To be able to say that each child is making appropriate progress in each year, we should be able to measure 12 months gain in any subject. If an age gain, such as one year in reading or spelling, isn't appropriate, they should be improving by a level or a stage in a curriculum area. If a third wave child is receiving good support through a full range of programmes and teaching interventions, we should see greater than chronological age progress. Ideally, this would be happening consistently if a child is to make up for past underachievement. These gains need to be measured and monitored through pre- and post-testing.

As we work through this process, I often have teachers say, 'In the past we were catering for mainstream, and third wave learners were disadvantaged. Now we are catering for third wave learners, and first and second wave learners are disadvantaged.'

This should never be the case. The learning and teaching pace should also be differentiated. If we focus on the developmental stages of learning, each student should be working at their development levels, at their own pace. A teacher will set learning and activities at each stage, and some self-directed activities and learning can even be set for more capable students. The class teacher shares their time between the students at the different stages. Trained teacher aides are used to support at-risk and slower learning groups, so they are always working at their optimum level. This style of teaching takes both skill and planning, but with experience, and the development of appropriate resources, it gets easier. With this approach, the positive outcomes and achievement increases markedly.

Some basic things we need to be aware of, when developing resources, are the needs of students with visual processing problems. Simple worksheets with larger print, clear spacing, bold headings and less information will be important. You may have five or six learners with this underpinning cognitive weakness. Have a ream of blue paper, or a suitably coloured paper, by the photocopier so that those who need it can have a modified resource. This is important to assist students with visual processing difficulties. Only doing it for those who need it minimises costs.

Some of the homework sheets that are made smaller, to squash more things on a smaller page, are overwhelming and totally unsuitable for third wave students. First and second wave learners may cope with this, and you can save paper. Differentiating for third wave students will always be necessary.

There will also need to be a focus on metacognitive strategies. These will need to be explicitly taught with lots of opportunity for practise. We will need to teach active revision skills, showing students how to review and summarise. The technique of scaffolding should be rigorously utilised, and there should be a focus on moving children from dependence to independence.

Often third wave children have difficulty getting started. At times, we may even find a lesson is fifteen minutes from the end, and you have got a few children that have hardly started. To minimise their fears of how to start, we can use several techniques. We can try giving paragraph starters or offer to act as a scribe for them to get their ideas flowing. We might organise them a buddy, we might do shared writing, or paired writing, and then eventually move to individual writing, so that we're supporting them along the process. We may get the buddy to do some, or all, of the writing. We may give them sentence starters and key words. We might use things like writing frames and skeleton plans. We might use thought showers and post-it notes. Thought showers were introduced to me as an alternative to brainstorming. Somebody thought 'storming the brain' was a bit violent, and showering thoughts was much better. I remember a group of us thought it was hilarious!

We will also want to accept work in a different form. By not always expecting things in a written form, we are not assessing children in their weak area. There is a very important concept here. Some people say that we make learning too easy for children with learning difficulties, we dumb down the education system and we give them too much support. Other people say that we don't do enough for children with learning difficulties and differences. Both statements may be true. Generally, parents and teachers have a certain expectation of a child depending on who they are. Usually, with good students we have high expectations, and with students who have learning difficulties, we have lower expectations. I believe we would do well to have two sets of expectations for children with learning difficulties. Firstly, we need to know these students really well, and be able to identify strengths and weaknesses. We would have high expectations in the areas of strength and communicate these. For example, 'You are an exceptional artist and sports person, and you are going to be a top achiever in these areas. I understand that you have difficulty with reading and writing, and we set realistic expectations for these areas.' This is greatly beneficial to children's self-esteem. Their areas of strength can be used to build their self-esteem. Very often, without this differentiated approach to achievement, children can have very poor self-belief and self-esteem, which can affect them all their lives.

In order to support children to reach their potential, we need to do two things. When we first find out that a child has a learning difficulty or difference, we need to put in place a whole range of support strategies to make life easier. For example, seat them up the front, provide buddy support, organise extra teacher aide time, having reduced homework expectations, etc. At the same time, we need to start teaching skills and strategies which assist the student to compensate and achieve, despite their difficulties. The whole world is not going to stop because they have a learning difficulty. By the time they reach upper levels in school, and go on into the workforce, they will need to have sufficient skills to cope in an adult world, and to achieve at a level that will bring them good outcomes. Our role in the primary years is to support a student, teach them skills to a sufficient level, and provide practise opportunities so the student can cope on their own. As skill level improves, we start withdrawing the support. By this method, we are scaffolding children to independence.

Many of these children fear information overload, and in fact, they do get overloaded. Our classrooms are very busy places. For many of these children, some of their underpinning cognitive weaknesses relate to sensory overload, so they can become overwhelmed in a classroom setting. I have some children who say to me, 'My brain feels like it's going to explode.' There is too much going on in a day. We have very busy curriculums. We have health people and programmes coming into school, we've got visiting artists, we've got field trips. We have the dental nurse, vision and hearing people, and whole school assessment practices. All these things create difficulties and add to third wave children feeling overloaded. We need to minimise this overloading as much as possible. When it is unavoidable, we need to understand and support students who are prone to anxiety, meltdowns, and behaviour problems, when this is going on.

We need to ensure we provide time for repetition to assist retention of learning. We will want to make instructions clear and concise, so as not to add to auditory overload. Giving one or two instructions at a time, and checking a student understands, is necessary. We can have instructions in a written form as well, which gives confirmation to auditory instructions and can be referred back to.

As class teachers, we need to encourage questions. This affirms an environment where it is good to ask for help or clarification. We need to smile and be enthusiastic, showing our willingness to help, and show we are interested in them as learners, even if at times we don't feel like it. We need to commit wholeheartedly to this philosophy as a sector. Students pick up very quickly if teachers aren't interested in them and haven't got time for them. These feelings impact negatively on achievement 100% of the time. As professionals, this is not something we want to take lightly.

Other strategies include marking spelling and content separately, so that we can keep children's thinking and ideas, which are their strengths, separate from their difficulties. We want to provide environments where there's lots of praise.

In particular we use descriptive praise. For example, 'I like the way that you summarised that. You used a mind map, and you highlighted keywords in colour. You will remember all this information because you used these strategies. Well done.'

We want to reduce the pressure and stress for children, because we know that stressed children, and children with anxiety, can't learn.

We also want to review learning at the beginning of each lesson. If you're interested in finding out more about this, I'd recommend reading the work of Mike Scaddan and his brain-compatible learning techniques.[22] He talks a lot about reviewing learning at the beginning of each lesson, as well as building on prior learning, using multisensory approaches to teaching and using a range of alternative strategies.

We need to establish the purpose for learning. We might state our learning intentions, and teach the metacognitive strategy, *Which strategy, why this strategy and how do I employ the strategy?*

It is my belief that the teaching and learning strategies that are outlined in this chapter should be evident in every classroom around the world. Until it is a part of basic philosophy and everyday teaching practice in education, we will be unable to meet the needs of at-risk learner groups. In order to support all teachers to up-skill and implement these strategies, it will need to be part of each school's mentoring and guidance approach. As schools develop policy and practice in this area, they will want to ensure that these types of ideas are part of every teacher's toolkit. To assist teachers and schools to develop and extend these ideas, refer to Appendix D for a checklist. I suggest that the checklist is used to measure the implementation of these concepts, as part of teacher self-evaluation and development, and later observation and appraisal. It can help to highlight any areas where further work is needed and provide the basis for discussion for professional development in areas where help is required. The goal here is ensuring that best practice becomes standard practice.

Chapter Eight

Underpinning Cognitive Weaknesses and the Value of Specialist Assessments

The next chapter is an extremely important one. It includes discussion on vision and learning difficulties. Some of you may have been told that vision problems are not the cause of dyslexia and that there is no research evidence to say that visual problems play a part in learning difficulties. Whilst there may be no current evidence that vision is the cause of learning difficulties there are many children who have learning difficulties and a visual problem. I urge you to explore the evidence for this and the research on vision and learning for yourself rather than discount it. In my experience if we do not address the visual problems identified alongside the phonological and other issues, we do not maximise achievement outcomes. If vision problems present themselves as an underpinning weakness, we can improve learning outcomes more quickly and effectively by addressing them.

As a teacher, one of the challenges for us is to look at how we've been operating in the classroom in the past. We have likely been focusing on academic programmes and perhaps overlooking underpinning cognitive weaknesses. Changing our thinking and our approach will be an area of challenge, and we will need to think of this time as a process of transition.

I remember when I was going through this process myself, it took me quite a while to see and understand the differences between second and third wave learners. As one of the directors for the SPELD New Zealand Certificate Course in Specific Learning Disabilities, I found that RTLBs, RTLits, SENCOs and teachers coming into that programme also took quite some time to make the leap or transition in thinking. It requires a shift in intention, from meeting the needs of mainstream children through focusing on academic subjects, to meeting the needs of third wave learners by understanding underpinning cognitive needs.

Part of this problem arises around terminology. Although we often have some idea of visual or auditory problems, our training didn't give us the background knowledge we require to fully understand or differentiate our teaching, so we could cater for these difficulties. For example, when we talk about visual processing, this is the process of the brain interpreting information taken in through sight. The difference between terms such as visual processing/perception and visual proficiency are often not well understood. When we look at a visual processing disorder, it refers to the difficulties of making sense of information that's taken in through the eyes, not whether the eyes see well. A student can have perfect vision but still have visual processing problems.

One of the key areas that cause difficulty is visual discrimination. This is the ability to differentiate objects based on their individual characteristics. Visual discrimination also refers to the ability to recognise an object as distinct from its surrounding environment. So, when we're looking at things like reading and mathematics, visual discrimination can interfere with their ability to accurately identify symbols, to get information from pictures, charts, or graphs, or to use visually presented material in a productive way.

Often children have trouble distinguishing between letter shapes. The letters *n* and *u*; *b* and *d*; *p* and *q*; as well as *m* and *w*, are often confused. The ability to recognise distinct shapes from their backgrounds, such as objects in a picture or letters on a chalk or whiteboard, are part of the visual discrimination problem.

Another underpinning cognitive weakness relates to visual memory. The person has difficulty remembering information from things that are seen. Extending on from that, they can have a visual sequential memory problem. This means that they have difficulty remembering things seen in order. It's a bit like not being able to find the right filing cabinet where the object or idea is stored. In education this can interfere with a child's ability to consistently recognise letters, numbers, symbols, words, or pictures. This can be very frustrating, because this also leads to performance inconsistency, where some days they have the information and other days they may not be able to retrieve the information.

For example, if you went on a field trip, and you were recalling the events on the field trip, you would have trouble sequencing the events. If you had seen a play or a show, and you were asked to recall the content of it, you would have trouble remembering the story line, or the events in sequence.

Visual figure ground and visual attention are closely related. Individuals with these difficulties have trouble focusing on the important thing in relation to other things.

For example, the teacher might be asking them to find some information from a poster that contains a lot of information. It is almost like, 'not being able to see the wood for the trees.' Another example is when a class teacher is speaking to a group of students, a child may be distracted by another group of students, who are talking on the other side of them. They might be distracted by the posters on the wall. They can't attend to the important thing.

Visual closure is another underpinning cognitive weakness. Visual closure is often considered to be related to visual discrimination. It is the ability to identify or recognise a symbol or object when the entire object is not visible. So, for example, difficulties with visual closure can be seen if a child is asked to identify or complete a drawing. If part of a drawing is missing, they have trouble seeing the whole of the picture. One of the reasons for this, is that children have an inability to integrate or synthesise visual stimuli into a recognisable whole. This can cause difficulties when new concepts are being taught. They may be able to grasp some aspects, but not get a true understanding of the full concept.

Visual spatial problems can also occur. This refers to the position of objects in space. It also refers to the ability to accurately perceive objects in space, with reference to other objects. In subjects like reading and maths, where accurate understanding of spatial relationships is important, this can cause problems. Because both subject areas rely heavily on the use of symbols, letters, and numbers; things like punctuation and math signs can be quite challenging for children who have difficulty with spatial problems. Here again, we see confusion between letter shapes, such as *B,b, D,d, P,p,* and *Q,q*. Do they go to the left, or do they go to the right?

The importance of being able to perceive objects in relation to other objects is often seen in math problems as well. For example, to be successful, the person must be able to associate that certain digits go together to make a single number, while other digits are single numbers by themselves. They must understand that the operational signs – for example, the addition, multiplication, and equals signs – are distinct from the numbers, but demonstrate a relationship between them. Children with visual spatial problems have difficulty with these concepts.

Finally, children may have difficulty with scanning and tracking, where the eyes don't coordinate well, to help them track across the page. To read well, it's important to have efficient tracking, and saccadic eye movements (the quick simultaneous movement of both eyes to jump quickly in the same direction between two or more points) working effectively. The eyes need to jump ahead, and scan back, to efficiently read the words. For children with visual scanning and tracking problems, this process isn't working well.

In chapter three, we got you to complete a reading task (see Appendix B). The content of the text was very important information and is given below.

> Reading is a very difficult task for people with learning difficulties. They say up to 70% of people with a learning disability have some kind of visual problem.[1,2,3,4] Often people have perfect vision, but their brain doesn't process what they see so well. Visual processing problems are very common, and these are not picked up through a normal eye test. Sometimes children skip words or add them when they are reading aloud, sometimes they miss lines, and make a lot of visual errors noted during running records. They can have visual sequencing problems, where they get the order of the letters or syllables out of order. Sometimes children complain that words move. Other times they aren't clear or are blurred. They often rub their eyes a lot and get tired easily. Children who exhibit these problems need to see a behavioural optometrist. There are not many in New Zealand, and the best thing to do is Google to find one in your area.

When we did our training, and particularly when we learnt how to do running records, we were taught to observe – and even record – much of the information contained in the paragraph above. Nobody told us that we actually needed to do something about these difficulties. I thought that through good teaching of reading that these problems would disappear. It wasn't until I did specialist training that I learned that this is not the case. If we observe signs of visual problems in our students during reading or general classwork, we need to investigate further.

Through this training, I became aware of the level of impact that visual processing problems have on learning. Visual processing problems are prevalent in students with learning difficulties. You will see from the text above that up to 70% of children with a learning difficulty have some kind of visual problem. The research is also showing that visual processing problems affect achievement in all academic subjects.[4] Over the last few years, I have been working with Stuart Warren in Auckland, and Ian Finch in the Bay of Plenty, to develop and implement visual training that enables visual problems to be identified and remediated by schools. With only a dozen or so behavioural optometrists in the country, many regions don't have ready access to a specialist. In addition, the cost of having needs addressed is prohibitive for many families. Getting a specialist assessment, paying for glasses if they are needed, and weekly visits to an optometrist for visual training for a period of time is costly. The cost of travel maybe an additional factor. Providing training for this is outside the scope of what we can do here. For those who are interested, I will put details at the back of the book regarding the online vision and learning programme.

For now, what I recommend is that you observe and take note of visual and visual processing problems in your students. Stuart Warren has designed an app called iCEPT, which you can download on your iPad free.[5] The app has four visual assessments and four auditory assessments. If you have concerns about your students, I suggest you put them through the iCEPT assessment. If they fail these assessments, this will confirm your thinking, and you can be sure when you make a referral to a behavioural optometrist that you are referring them to the right place. Be sure to refer to a behavioural optometrist, rather than a normal optometrist. Behavioural optometrists do the work of a usual optometrist, but they also cover vision and learning/processing problems. I have had many children who have seen a normal optometrist and been told their eyes are fine, but they still have vision and learning problems, and end up being diagnosed later with visual processing problems. It is common to have perfect 20/20 vision, but still have a visual processing problem.

Auditory processing problems are also very common in children. Just as we have the number and variety of problems in the visual area, we can have similar problems with auditory processing. Auditory processing interferes with an individual's ability to analyse or make sense of information which is taken in through the ears.

This is not a hearing problem. People with auditory processing problems may have excellent hearing, but their ears don't process or interpret what they hear well. This is why we can have many children who have had a school or audiologist hearing check, and come back with a good report but still have processing difficulties in these areas undetected.

An auditory processing deficit can interfere directly with speech and language, but it can affect all areas of learning, especially reading and spelling. One of the areas that many of the children have problems with is phonological awareness. These problems occur around the understanding that language is made up of individual sounds, and that the smallest units of sounds, which are phonemes, are put together to form words that we write and speak. Having this knowledge is vital in reading and spelling, and children with this problem are unable to recognise and isolate the individual sounds in words. They also have difficulty recognising similarities and differences between words. They have trouble recognising and creating rhyme, and they also have difficulty with onset and rime. These deficits can affect all areas, including reading, writing and understanding of spoken language. It would be fair to say that most children who have a learning difficulty have got a phonological/phonemic weakness.

Auditory discrimination problems are very common. This is the ability to recognise the difference in phonemes and sounds.

Children may have trouble hearing the difference between the vowel sounds: *a, e, i, o,* and *u*. This includes the ability to identify words and sounds that are similar, and those that are different.

These children also have auditory memory difficulties, where just like with vision, they have difficulty remembering what is heard. They have trouble storing and recording information which is given verbally.

An individual with difficulties in this area may not be able to follow instructions given verbally, and they may have trouble recalling information from a story that's read aloud.

Auditory sequencing is the ability to remember or reconstruct the order of items, e.g. in a list, an order of events, or the order of sounds in a word or a syllable. We get lots of children who say, 'hopsitals', 'aminals' and 'emenies'. All the syllables are there, but in the wrong order.

Auditory figure ground is when children have difficulty selecting the important thing to pay attention to, when there are other competing sounds. So again, hearing and interpreting the class teacher's voice when there is noise in the classroom, when there are other children speaking, when there's a phone ringing in the background, or when two adults are talking. They have trouble attending to auditory stimuli.

Auditory closure is another underpinning cognitive weakness. This is where a child has trouble interpreting what is said, when they don't hear a complete word or idea. For children, this can be quite a major problem. Once we get older, we have a large word bank. If we lose our hearing or we start to go deaf in old age, because we have a very strong word bank, we can often understand partially heard words and sentences, because we can link the part of what we heard to our memory. For children who are still developing their knowledge of vocabulary, this word base isn't as strong, so auditory closure can be a problem.

Processing speed is also a common underpinning difficulty. Processing speed involves the ability to complete relatively simple cognitive tasks with automaticity. Possible implications of this are that children may have difficulty processing information rapidly, or they have difficulty completing assignments within time limits. They often have difficulty taking timed tests, particularly maths mental tests. I've had quite a few parents talk to me about the difficulty of such tests, and how stressful it is for their children, who have processing speed difficulties, to complete timed tests. Making rapid comparisons between and among pieces of information and copying problems can also create difficulties, when speed or time is a factor.

Short term memory involves the ability to hold information in mental awareness and to use it within a few seconds. This may be influenced by attention. Difficulty following directions is also a challenge for many of these students. They have trouble remembering information long enough to process it for understanding. They may have trouble recalling sequences, with memorising information, and in listening to and comprehending lengthy texts. They'll have difficulty taking notes. Working memory difficulties often show up in subjects like maths, where you've got to remember information, and manipulate that information to work with it.

Finally, two common underpinning cognitive weaknesses concern gross and fine motor skills. Some children have difficulty with coordination, managing large limbs and moving in a coordinated way, which affects them in sports. It also affects their rhythm and balance. Other children have problems with their fine motor skills, which creates difficulty with writing, as well as gluing, sticking, cutting and colouring in. It is also recognised that children with gross and fine motor skill difficulties have poor left–right brain integration. Children with poor left–right brain integration are more at risk for learning difficulties.[6]

Now that we have a basic understanding of underpinning cognitive weaknesses, the next step is to look at how can we use specialist assessment to identify these underpinning cognitive weaknesses, and identify the strengths that children have. This is potentially a very important topic. There's a lot of debate in schools whether there is a need for specialist assessments at all. In the past it has been recognised that these are necessary at a high school level. In exams, these tests are important to justify Special Assessment Conditions (SAC), and to determine whether students qualify for assistant readers, writers and extra time. More recently the rules have been relaxed to allow in-school staff to make applications for Special Assessment Conditions using a variety of different tools and evidence. This is essentially a very good thing, because the cost of assessments for this purpose have ranged from $450 to $1000, and the cost of this often falls to parents. As a result, children who often needed SAC did not get them, which has resulted in inequity in the support for at-risk students.

If we set aside the need for SAC, there has often been little consideration towards whether a specialist assessment is needed. Both as a teacher and a parent, I believe that these assessments are very necessary. As a teacher, many of the assessments we do in schools are focused on academic areas. They do not look at any underpinning cognitive weaknesses that a child may have that is preventing them from learning and achievement.

Before we can decide on the best intervention, we need to determine the needs. In general, my experience has been that we do a lot of excellent assessment in schools. However, what is done is largely meeting the needs of first and second wave learners, and perhaps fourth wave learners. As a specialist and a professional, I feel we have underestimated the value of specialist assessments. There are several reasons why we would want to use a specialist assessment.

Firstly, we want to be able to identify the underpinning cognitive weaknesses that a child has. As a classroom teacher, I can observe certain things about a child, and I could probably even identify quite a few of the areas where a child has an underpinning cognitive weakness. But I'm unlikely to be able to determine the extent of these in sufficient detail to devise an adequate programme. When I have a specialist assessment, it gives me a list of all the underpinning cognitive weaknesses, and it also shows me whether they are a mild, moderate or major difficulty.

Secondly, an assessment identifies the strengths that a child has. And when I know those strengths, I can use those to support learning. For example, if I identify that the child has an auditory strength, but they have a visual weakness, I can use the auditory modality to support their learning, and develop their visual weaknesses.

The other thing that's interesting relates to IQ. Whilst IQ is not regarded as a factor in diagnosis, the assessments show whether the child has above average intelligence, average intelligence, or is below average in intelligence. Whatever a person's intelligence level is, all their academic scores should sit around about their intelligence level. In the case of specific learning difficulties, what we find is that some children have very low scores in some areas, and in some areas, they can have very high scores. There are unexpected differences in their ability.

Frequently, I get reports back, and we can have children who may be 14 years of age and they can have scores in some areas that are as low as 8–9 year olds, and then they can have some scores that are equivalent to 15 year olds or greater, in other areas.

As a teacher, this is quite difficult to grasp. When we do assessments, we won't often see those discrepancies in a child's learning ability. The benefit of having this knowledge is that we can design appropriate programmes to meet an identified, specific need. The other thing that is very sad, is that many of the children that I come across feel quite confused about themselves. On the one hand, they know that they have a good brain, and then in other ways, they wonder, 'How come I can't do these basic, simple things?' Left unaddressed, these problems compound, and can cause behaviour problems and result in children not achieving their potential.

Once children have an assessment, and have this explained, they understand what is going on for them. It improves their confidence and self-esteem, sometimes dramatically. They are now able to say, 'These are my weaknesses, this is what I've got to work on, and I'm good at these things.'

As a classroom teacher who has had specialist training, I am able to design and deliver a much better programme if I have this information. As a specialist teacher, I can target specific weaknesses, and utilise strengths, to support this teaching. Whilst I am likely to make some progress without a specialist assessment, we can achieve far greater results in a shorter space of time with a specialist assessment.

I had an interesting conversation with a colleague recently. She said she has been unsure about schools requesting a specialist assessment. She wanted to know, 'What will a school do differently if it has a specialist assessment?'

She asks a very good question. I have always been pro specialist assessments. I use them to inform teaching, such as designing an IEP, putting in accommodations, and identifying strategies and skills that need teaching, and highlighting strengths. Another reason I have always recommended them is if a family plans to have a specialist teacher, like someone from SPELD, to target teach.

However, because we don't give training in this area, many teachers, SENCOs, and even RTLBs and RTLits, have difficulty interpreting assessments, and they are not used to their full capacity. My view is that rather than discouraging people from getting assessments done, we need to train every educator to interpret them, and how to use them to raise achievement and improve outcomes. Sadly, I must admit that many parent dollars have been spent, only to have assessments sit in a filing cabinet, and not used to make a difference to a child's learning.

Parents are likely to try a range of interventions, such as tutoring agencies like Kip McGrath, Number Works, or private tutors, etc. Tutoring outside school is fraught with the same difficulties as in school programmes. Many programmes are very good, but if you use a second wave programme to support a third wave learner, you are going to be disappointed and waste money. If a specialist assessment is done, then we can select the best approach based on the assessment findings. Kip McGrath, Number Works and private tutors, etc., can achieve great outcomes for low literacy or underachieving students. However, unless the programmes and tutors focus on underpinning weaknesses rather than academic programmes, they are unsuitable for third wave students.

In some cases, we have non-teachers purchasing learning franchises. They are trained in that programme, but have little to no understanding of learning difficulties outside the programmes they have been trained in. I am a member of a few Facebook groups, and I am regularly embarrassed about some of the things I read, some of the things people are told, and the lack of understanding and plethora of misinformation that is out there. I reiterate that some of the tutoring programmes are good, but they are generally for underachieving, low literacy, mainstream students, not for third wave learners. One of the tragedies about this situation is that every time a student tries a programme and doesn't succeed, it adds to their feeling of failure. Many of these students have tried several programmes, and they are still well below their chronological age in their achievement, and they know it. Children's self-worth, and belief in themselves as a learner, plummets in these situations. I have apologised to many children about the experience they have had in education. I believe the system has failed the children, rather than the children failing the system.

In my experience, just as schools have spent funds on inappropriate interventions, so have parents. My advice to parents who say they can't afford an assessment, but are prepared to pay a weekly tutor, is do nothing for a term, to save your money and then get the report done. In the meantime, we often look for other funding options. We have had a number of schools pay for assessments, we have had RTLB cluster funding pay or subsidise some assessments. People like SPELD and other organisations will often offer subsidies, and I have even had church groups and other philanthropic agencies cover costs.

If we accept that testing is important, we then need to consider which type of test will be most beneficial. There are a number of different tests that can be used. Traditionally, we've used the Weschler Intelligence Scale for Children (WISC) assessments which are intelligence type assessments that are completed by trained psychologists. These tests measure children's IQ and their cognitive ability. SPELD New Zealand was involved in a great deal of research, and worked collaboratively with several key people, including James Chapman from Massey University, looking into the available assessments worldwide. In the past, SPELD had developed their own SPELD battery assessments, which had been used for many years. Around 2002, it was felt that this assessment had been superseded, and what was needed was a reputable standardised assessment, which was internationally consistent and that had validity.

It was decided that the Woodcock-Johnson, which is an internationally recognised test, would be the most suitable.[7] One of the benefits is that it offers both a cognitive assessment, which is an IQ test, and also an academic and achievement assessment. The combination of these two assessments, the cognitive and the achievement, give a very clear picture of a child's performance academically.

Currently we are having quite a few people, like the Infant Child Adolescent Mental Health Service (ICAHMs), using WISC IQ assessment and referring children on to get a full educational assessment, like the Woodcock-Johnson completed.

In education, we value the model which allows for a pre-test, quality intervention and a post-test. I believe that the Woodcock-Johnson provides this well. By identifying needs through a pre-test, remediating underpinning cognitive weaknesses, and then utilising the Woodcock-Johnson as a post-test, we can demonstrate measurable changes in student achievement that we have not been able to achieve to date in mainstream education for these students. These findings have been replicated in a recent independent study, a pilot project led by Karen Waldie at Auckland University, undertaken for SPELD New Zealand.[8]

The cost of these assessments is one of the most prohibitive challenges we need to overcome if we are to support children, their families, class teachers, specialist teachers and schools to truly address the needs of at-risk students.

As parents, we have paid for three assessments for our son. The first time was to get a diagnosis, the second time was to monitor progress of specialist teaching and the third time was to assist with a SAC application. I understand this is a challenge for parents, but parents often spend a lot of money on interventions that may not necessarily provide good outcomes. In the long run, getting this done helps us spend money in the right places.

The cost of assessments can be particularly prohibitive for low-income families. I reiterate that in New Zealand, some 'not for profits' will subsidise, some philanthropic organisations and church groups also pay for some students. Some schools allow parents to put it on a school account and pay it off, and sometimes government agencies pay for low-income families. Whilst funding is an important consideration, a solution can often be found.

There are two key points to take from this chapter. Firstly, an understanding of underpinning cognitive weaknesses, and how these can be the root cause of a child's failure to achieve. Secondly, an understanding of specialist's assessments, and how these can give you valuable insights into a child's learning needs, and how teaching and learning can be enhanced.

Chapter Nine

Determining the Next Steps for My Students

If we consider the waves in learning, we are likely to have a mix of all students in our class. A few students may be gifted and require extension. The majority of the students will be mainstream. We are likely to have five or six students who are third wave, and perhaps one or two who fit into the special education category. Our role as classroom teacher gives us the primary responsibility of ensuring we meet all these students' needs, and that we support them well, raising achievement and assisting them to reach their potential.

In all these student groups we can have groups within groups, and even students who can be two waves at the same time. For example, 10–15% of students will be gifted and also have a learning difficulty.[1] Often these students are not achieving to potential, and their giftedness gets overlooked, because they are performing as a student in the mainstream group.

Within the mainstream second wave group, we may have students above average and working a bit above their chronological age, we may have students who are achieving at age, and we may also have students who are achieving six months to two years below their chronological age. I call these low literacy students. These students, due to a range of barriers to learning, are underachieving. These barriers can include attendance problems, children who are transient and have families who move a lot, children with health problems, children with home background difficulties and children who, for one reason or another, haven't had adequate opportunity to learn.

We may also have children who are third and fourth wave, at the same time. These children may have sensory, intellectual or physical problems, but also have a learning difficulty or ADHD at the same time.

When we look at the range of students in our classes, it is not surprising that being trained as a mainstream teacher is not adequate to do this job well. Classifying our children in to first, second, third and fourth wave learners is the first step to ensuring we recognise and understand their needs. Appendix E is a template to allow you to place your students in the various waves. When you complete this exercise, think of this as the first draft. As you go through the process in this chapter, you may decide you need to make changes. In chapter two, we discussed characteristics of children with learning differences and difficulties, and we looked at a checklist of characteristics (see Appendix A). Based on what you already know about your students, and looking at the checklist, place them into learning waves using the model. Go ahead and do this now, and then come back to this page.

An important step is to differentiate between low literacy second wave students, and third wave students, so we want to find out which students have underpinning cognitive weaknesses. We are looking for weaknesses in the six following areas: visual processing, auditory processing, short term and working memory, processing delays, phonological awareness and gross and fine motor skills. To undertake this next step can be challenging. Our training as mainstream teachers taught us to assess academic achievement, and to use the information diagnostically to inform our teaching, but we were not trained to look for underpinning weaknesses. Without identifying and addressing underpinning weaknesses, children continue to underachieve, despite a range of interventions that have already been tried.

When teachers and other educators, myself included, first embark on this pathway, we all find it difficult to transition from being a mainstream teacher to a specialist third wave teacher. Think of this as a journey. The organisation I represent offers online one-year mentoring programmes to assist teachers with their development in this area.[2] I often find that schools and teachers think they can do some short professional development in this area, and be equipped for the role. Once they get into it, they realise just how much there is to learn, and that it takes experience to be successful in this area of education. The difference between a doctor who is a GP, and a doctor who is a specialist, is huge. You wouldn't expect to become a specialist without considerable further training, but often we don't apply the same philosophy to specialist teaching. Thankfully, it doesn't take years to do this work, usually one year of development and training is needed. The information and tools in this book will go a long way to getting you started on this journey. Should you decide that you would like to have a coach in this journey, you can refer to the information at the back of the book regarding Raising Achievement's one-year online mentoring programmes.

We need a screening tool to assist us with identifying underpinning weaknesses. Over the years, I have put together a series of assessments, from a range of sources, that we find very successful for this purpose. At Raising Achievement,[2] we use – and recommend – this screening tool for all our courses.

A digital copy of the written summary on conducting screening assessments, some useful resources and templates are available electronically on request and are listed at the end of the Appendices section.

One of the key resources and teaching tools I have used most in my specialist career is 'Alpha to Omega', by Hornsby, Shear and Pool.[3] It is an integrated reading, writing and spelling programme that you will hear a lot more about later, in chapter eleven. It is a handbook for phonological and spelling teaching. The initial assessment tool at the front of the book is the first assessment we use. Also in our kit is an adapted Midland Spelling Scale, which is completed as a dictation test.

The Midland Spelling Scale, we understand, is an obsolete spelling assessment which gave a rudimentary spelling age. The adaptation is that it is used as a dictation assessment, primarily for the purpose of identifying underpinning cognitive weaknesses rather than giving a definitive spelling achievement age. To be used effectively as part of the screening tool, a series of dictation sentences are given which students have to write. The adapted test, when analysed, provides information on auditory and visual difficulties, processing delays, short term and working memory and additional information on phonological and letter–sound pattern weaknesses.

The third assessment we recommend is a PROBE reading comprehension assessment.[4] We use this tool to find underpinning visual weaknesses in addition to the usual running records, measuring decoding and comprehension skills. A ten-minute writing sample is the fourth part of our approach, and we use a numeracy interview to complete the series of assessments,[5] which will give us an understanding of the underpinning weaknesses that are affecting each student. For junior students reading under the age of 7 years, we also use the assessment from an oral language programme, *Hei Awhiawhi Tamariki ki te Panui Pukapuka* (HPP).[6] We will also discuss this programme in chapter eleven.

These assessments are not the only assessments that can be used. Whatever assessments are used, they must be focused on identifying underpinning weaknesses, not academic achievement. The Alpha to Omega text with assessment will need to be purchased, along with the PROBE assessment. I want to unpack each of the assessments now, outlining how it is undertaken, how it is marked and the information you can extract from it.

Alpha to Omega Assessment[3]

Whilst it is possible to use a different phonological-spelling-patterns assessment, this is the one I recommend. Alpha to Omega teaches spelling patterns following the developmental stages of children's learning. Other programmes that I have used, and are often used by schools, are good programmes but they often suit mainstream learners better. They go too fast for our third wave learners, and introduce too many sounds too quickly, and often together. I have had many schools report they have tried a number of programmes with their at-risk and priority learners, without sufficient progress. When they change to Alpha to Omega for these students, progress and achievement increases markedly.

The assessment involves 78 words, which follow the developmental stages of learning patterns. These progress from short vowels, to long vowels, and on to blends, digraphs, triple blends, assimilation, *ng/nk* pattern, *ar/or/er* pattern, *w* rules, etc. All in all, the first stage of this programme covers the first 30 letter patterns that children learn. When we mark this test, we are more concerned with the students' knowledge of the letter patterns, than whether they get the word right or wrong. So, when we mark the test, we will have a series of sounds and letter patterns that the student is yet to master. It is expected that the first 30 patterns should be mastered by children before the age of 8 years. The errors made form a summary of the assessment, and the basis of the teaching programme.

In addition to highlighting a child's spelling and phonological difficulties, a lot can be picked up regarding auditory and visual processing problems, as well as processing delays. For example, children who write 'tab', instead of 'tub', or 'frush', instead of 'thrush', have auditory discrimination problems, where they are not hearing the differences between sounds accurately. Children with auditory memory problems may not be able to retain the word they are being asked to spell, after you put it in a sentence. Children with visual discrimination difficulties may write 'dag', for 'bag', or 'flod', for 'flop'. Children with visual sequencing problems may get all the right letters, but in the wrong order, spelling 'hepl' instead of 'help', or 'slpash' instead of 'splash'. Children with visual spatial problems may have uneven letter sizes, write uphill or downhill, or not start writing by the margin. It is important not to give children a piece of paper with grid lines for this assessment, and use just a piece of normal lined paper for their age. If you use grid lined paper, although it will be easier to mark, the visual spatial underpinning weakness won't show up. You can also observe things like whether children form letters correctly and whether they have an appropriate pencil grip. Even fine motor skill problems can be noted by the way they write and use the pencil. It is important to pick up children who have processing delays, and take longer than others to complete the test.

As a class teacher I would complete this assessment with my whole class at once, but I would wander around the class during the test and make notes as I observe difficulties in students. As a teacher, I need to know where all my students are at, in terms of phonological knowledge / letter–sound patterns and spelling. If I have students who are beyond this stage, they can go on to stage 2 or 3 of the programme, but I need to know whether children have gaps in their learning and where teaching for every child should begin. It is not necessary to complete the whole test, especially for younger children. As I walk around, if I can see a child has four or five letter pattern errors and is having difficulty, I will say that they can stop. I will continue for others that can go further. It is important to protect children's self-esteem, and not let them continue if you have the information that you need from the assessment.

Adapted Midland Spelling Scale

The next assessment is the adapted Midland Spelling scale, which I would also do with my whole class. The assessment gives you information on spelling, up to the age of 14 years. There are nineteen sentences which are read out twice. There is no time limit on the test, but do note children who have processing delays, and take longer than others. Based on the ages of the students in my class, I will usually go one year beyond their chronological age, although you can go further if you want to assess the good spellers' levels. You will see from the test, for example, that a 9 year old should be able to spell protection, motion and frighten. If I wanted to stop at a 10 year old level, I would stop after sentence twelve. If I am in a class setting, I will say, 'If you are 9 and would like to stop now, you can.' I would then carry on. Then I would say, 'If you are 10 and would like to stop now, you can.' I would continue like this until all the ages in the class had been reached.

When marking the assessment, you are looking for all the underpinning cognitive weaknesses noted when we marked Alpha to Omega. Although the test is completed as a dictation, we only mark the underlined words. I usually tick the words correct and circle the errors. You add up the correct words, and then compare it to the table. A 9 year old spelling age means twenty-one words are correct. Sometimes students may get one or two right in the next age, and you will need to make a teacher judgement about half years. On other occasions, you may get a child who makes early errors, but gets later words correct. You will need to make a best-fit teacher judgement here also. Remember, the main point of this is to determine underpinning weaknesses, but it will also be useful for pre- and post-testing to have a spelling age.

PROBE Reading Comprehension Assessment[4]

The next assessment we use is a PROBE reading comprehension assessment. Many schools already have this resource. It is important that you have had training in its use, and that it is used correctly. I will make some comments about this throughout this section, but do ensure you have good knowledge of the assessment before you use it. If you don't already have a kit, these can be purchased from Triune Initiatives Ltd.

The first part of the assessment is the PROBE Determiner. This is a test of a student's ability to read random words, and gives you information on decoding ability. Whilst the student is reading each set, take note of any visual problems, such as difficulty with word endings, or reading letters out of order. Allow the students to continue reading each set, until you hear a change in their voice, or hesitations. This is usually an indication that the words are approaching the end of their comfort zone. I then stop them, and ask a few questions relating to various word meanings. I also ask them at this point that when they look at words, are the words clear (not blurry). I ask them if the text is still, or if the words move. You will be amazed at how many children tell you words are blurry and / or move, and how many times you pick up visual problems.

From here we will select a text level for the student to read, based on our judgement from the Determiner. Remember again, here we are aiming to identify underpinning weaknesses, and next steps in teaching, rather than determining a reading age for the student. Allow the child to read the text to themselves. Then have the child read it out loud and score it as a running record. Ensure you are fully conversant with conventional running record scoring. There is some information on this in the manual that comes with PROBE if you need clarification or training for this.

Ask the child the questions, and advise them that they are allowed to look back at the text. They are not required just to remember from the reading. Write down the students answers exactly as they say them. Make any notes you wish to on the answer sheet regarding things you observe. Marking the assessment will involve counting errors and self-corrections, and determining a percentage level for decoding. You will also make notes about speed, hesitations, omissions, insertions and the student's level of dependence. When marking, you must use the marking guide and answers from the manual. No half-marks are allowed, and you must follow the justifications for answers, as the marking guide outlines. This will give you a comprehension score/percentage, and also indicate where a child needs comprehension development. This will be discussed in greater depth in the programmes section in chapter eleven.

Writing Sample

The next assessment is a ten-minute writing sample, which I would also do with the whole class. Some schools do a twenty-minute sample, which is also fine. We don't want to do more assessment than we need to. The key thing here is that it is unassisted. You can say to children that they can spend some time planning, and then they will write. One or two minutes before the end, you can say that they have two minutes left which they may want to use for editing. I usually say to children that you can write on any topic you like, but I also give a few topics for children who find that too broad and can't choose. I always use the same three options.

- **My experience of school so far.**
- **The best holiday I ever had.**
- **Last night I had the strangest dream.**

For the marking of the writing sample, we use the Assessment Resource Bank (ARB) tool.[7] It is simple to use. You can level children for both surface and deeper features. It assists you with next teaching steps, and it can give you a lot of information on underpinning weaknesses.

Numeracy Project Assessment[5]

The last assessment is numeracy. Numeracy assessments are excellent at highlighting processing delays, and short term and working memory difficulties. An interview is used, because it gives you the best understanding of a child's mathematical thinking, whether they can hold numbers in their head and manipulate them, and whether they have processing delays in number knowledge. We prefer to use the Numeracy Project Assessment (NumPA) diagnostic tool,[8] as it gives us a very good indication of underpinning cognitive weaknesses. Some schools use GloSS,[9] or Jam,[10] and I appreciate that for whole class use, this is quicker. If you are confident you can get the information about short term and working memory and processing delays with the assessment you use, this will be fine. I suggest you at least use NumPA for your third wave / at-risk students.

Ensure you record the students answers fully, so you can evaluate the answers for marking and comparing thinking development for the future. Also, don't give students pen and paper for this assessment. Once you give them pen and paper, you are unable to see if they have short term and working memory difficulties, and / or processing delays.

I recommend you complete all five assessments with your students. This way you can gain an overall picture of your students. As a class teacher, it is likely that you will want to do the complete assessment for five to ten students. You may want to include those who you think are low literacy underachievers, to ensure they don't have underpinning cognitive weaknesses also. By completing the Alpha to Omega, Midland Spelling Scale and ten-minute writing sample with your whole class, you gain valuable diagnostic information to assist you with programme planning and teaching. You will also want to do numeracy assessments and running records with your whole class, but I recommend you do the at-risk students first. This information will be needed before you can design a programme that will impact achievement, whereas general teaching and following curriculum year objectives will support your other students until you gain more information. Wherever you identify visual processing problems, complete the iCEPT visual and auditory assessments discussed earlier, to give you further information.

When you first start doing these assessments, they do take time, but with experience you will get quicker. Plot your class data so you have an assessment summary. If you want to add any other assessments, or you complete the HPP assessment,[6] you can add columns to a base template.

Once you have completed your at-risk students table you will be able to make decisions about any specialist referrals you wish to make. You will largely be selecting from behavioural optometrist, audiologist, Child Adolescent Mental Health Service (CAMHS), or a paediatrician for children with characteristics of ADHD, children on the autism spectrum, or those with signs of dyspraxia. For specific learning difficulties, a specialist educational assessor will be needed. In New Zealand, SPELD New Zealand trains and supports specialist assessors in the Woodcock-Johnson assessment, which provides both the intellectual and academic assessment we are looking for. There are also some private psychologists that work with the Woodcock-Johnson assessment.

In addition to any specialist assessments, your students will need an adapted classroom programme, as well as third wave programmes and approaches. Fortunately, these programmes will benefit all students, so the work you put into developing these will benefit everybody. Individual and group learning plans, accommodations and programmes will be discussed in following chapters.

Chapter Ten

Accommodations, Strategies and Individual Learning Plans

When we first find out a student has a learning difficulty, it is important for us to devise accommodations. Accommodations are any supports that assist a student to cope in the classroom. This could be seating a child up the front, facing the teacher, to assist with auditory problems. It could be seating a child at the side of the room, so they can get up and move and giving them a fidget toy to cater for ADHD. It may be giving a child a skeleton plan to assist with a writing task. Accommodations, on their own, are not going to solve the problem. It is also important that we teach skills and strategies to help students address the problems for themselves. In our teaching training, we were commonly taught that our role is to move children from dependence to independence. This concept applies to children with learning difficulties very strongly. When children first find out they have a learning difficulty, we need to put in place accommodations to support them in the classroom. At the same time, we need to teach skills, strategies and programmes to help them overcome the difficulties, thus moving them from dependence to independence. What often happens is that we put in accommodations, without doing the remediation with skills and strategies. When this happens, we get secondary school students reaching exam stage, still dependent on accommodations, and who don't have the skills to tackle higher level education. They are unprepared for increasing independence in life.

We have already spoken about the need for early identification, but another reason that this is so vital is that we have the primary years to help students understand their learning differences, difficulties or disabilities. In this time, we can assist them with skills and tools to remediate them, so they can read and write well enough to access the curriculum when they go to secondary school. Sadly, we are seeing far too many students entering secondary school with curriculum attainment at levels of 4, 3 and even 2. This is far lower than the level 5 and 6 needed for success. Over recent years, I am finding myself working with secondary schools who have many children entering year 9 with undiagnosed learning difficulties. This means, if we identify them in the first term of year 9, that we have only two years to do much of the work to prepare them for NCEA. This could have and should have been done prior to year 8.

I have always said that we have done the best we can in education with the knowledge and the resources we have had. Over the last five to ten years, we have learned so much about the brain. We have increasing knowledge of best practice, and we have historical achievement data to work with. All this data and information points to a relatively large group of students, for whom we are not doing very well within our traditional mainstream education approach. Rather than be critical of the past, it is time to recognise this systemic failure, to learn from the past and to make positive change in education so as to provide equity for all groups. If we can equip schools and individual teachers with the skills and knowledge of early identification, the tools for remediation, and a robust system for monitoring and measuring performance, we will be able to rectify this situation.

We now know that we can identify signs and characteristics of children at risk in preschool. In the past, we have often said that some children have developmental delays, and they are not ready for school, so we have tended to wait until little Johnny is 6 and then say, 'Oh dear. He's not reading very well, we better give him a Reading Recovery programme.' We now know the skills children need. We know that children with good phonological awareness go on to later success. We know children need rhyme recognition, rhyme creation and onset ('beginning') and rime ('ending', not rhyme). We also know that children who speak well go on to success in later reading and writing. We have some fabulous programmes like Hei Awhiawhi Tamariki ki te Panui Pukapuka (HPP),[1] with proven success for advancing children in all these areas. We have researched data that shows it is a programme that provides good results for our Maori and Pasifika students, and it is a programme that can be started at as young as 3 years of age. Our past approach has been very much an ambulance at the bottom of the cliff, rather than building fences at the top. Programmes like PMP – the Perceptual Motor Programme –[2] and quality preschool programmes, including things like tumble gym and preschool music, assist in supporting our children through the necessary development stages to prepare them for school and an academic education.

Preschool education is outside the scope of this book.

What we do want to do is equip all educators in the school setting to identify and meet the needs of all school entrants, from the time they walk in the door, and support them to success as they move through the years, and successfully leave with school qualifications. Already, much of this book has been about giving every teacher the knowledge and skills to understand and identify students. Our next steps will be the action we need to take to ensure the outcomes change.

Once we have the understanding, and have completed the assessments, whether we have a diagnosis or not, we need to consider accommodations. We are looking for accommodations in each of the identified cognitive weaknesses. Often, if we have a specialist assessment done, there will be a section in the report on appropriate accommodations for the classroom. I have always found it very useful to have a list of accommodations for each weak area identified. For ready reference, we will now go through a range of accommodations. The key thing to remember here is that accommodations are only one part of the equation. They are important, and used while skills and strategies are developing. We start withdrawing them as skill level increases. For example, we may use sentence starters, word banks, writing frames and skeleton plans to support a child while they are learning the process of writing, but these things are withdrawn as the child strengthens their own skills. By year 11, at the very latest, they need to be confident writers and be able to structure quality text and write essays unassisted.

Definition of accommodations – these are supports/strategies offered in the classroom to enhance learning achievement for at-risk students.

Processing Delays

- **Giving extra time for tasks**
- **Reduce quantity of work in favour of quality**
- **Give reader/writer for tests and exams**
- **Limit or structure copying from board or other copying activities.**

Comprehension Knowledge

- **Give trigger words**
- **Give prior knowledge needed, e.g. through pictures, vocab list**

- Link new learning to previous learning
- Use multisensory teaching, mind maps/diagrams/ YouTube etc.

Basic Reading

- Reader/writer assistant
- Audio texts
- High interest/easy reading
- Ensure reading at correct level
- Assign a buddy reader.

Phonemic Awareness

- Seat students in front of teacher so they have visual (can see teacher's face) as well as auditory contact
- Give spelling lists divided into syllables
- Give spelling lists as word families
- Provide alphabet cards.

Fluid Reasoning

- Break down complex problems into parts
- Chunk activities
- Give concrete materials to work with

- **Give real life scenarios when introducing new concepts.**

Writing Difficulties

- **Allow use of a word processor – use spell-check**
- **Teach strategies – mind mapping, brain storming, note taking, thought showers, graphic organisers**
- **For phoneme-grapheme problems, mark written work for quality of ideas**
- **To assist hand eye co-ordination and improve handwriting use a ruler and a washed out highlighter to guide the student in the writing process showing where the small letters go as shown in the diagram below .**

The following image is used with permission from Neil McKay.[3]

Memory

Short Term Retrieval –

- **Limit oral instructions**
- **Use visual and kinaesthetic prompts**
- **Give clear, precise instructions.**

Long Term Retrieval –

- **Strategy/rule cards to recall certain methods**
- **Cue cards**
- **Assisting devices – Ready Reckoners, spell checks, calculators**
- **Open book exams and tests**
- **More opportunities to practise and review**
- **Games and activities for overlearning**
- **Metacognitive strategies for memory – mnemonics, mind maps, etc.**

Visual Memory

- **Write spelling list straight in their notebook, or give written copy**
- **Limit copying**
- **Give verbal cues.**

Maths Calculation Skills

- **Multiplication chart or table**
- **Calculators**
- **Use of manipulatives or concrete materials**
- **Giving real life scenarios**

- **Multisensory learning – visual, auditory and kinaesthetic modalities.**

Directionality

- **Mark starting point for writing with an agreed symbol**
- **Provide a guide – ruler or card**
- **Give cues, e.g. you wear your watch on your left hand.**

Auditory Processing

- **Provide brief, simple and clear oral instructions**
- **Seat at front of class**
- **Check in system with teacher or buddy for clarification.**

Oral Language

- **Allow extra time to respond or speak**
- **Give prior warning when you will ask them to speak**
- **Limit length of instructions**
- **Use concrete examples and demonstrations, use visuals, hand gestures**
- **Develop key vocabulary for new subject content.**

Proprioception

- **Give squeezable ball**
- **Use triangle shaped pencil or pencil grip**
- **Allow student to lean on a wall at mat time**
- **Teach proper posture, and give support and encouragement.**

Visual Figure Ground

- **Provide plain worksheets – lots of white space**
- **Larger print, bold key words, pastel paper.**

When we begin to consider the programmes and strategies we use, these should all be based on the seven key excellences in teaching for third wave students that we discussed in chapter five. To recap, these are:

1) Multisensory teaching
2) Structured programmes
3) Sequential and based on the developmental stages of learning
4) Based in neuroscience and research, best practice
5) Utilising repetition and overlearning
6) Based on diagnostic evidence
7) Explicitly teaching metacognitive strategies.

Our next step is to consider the planning for change that needs to occur for individuals and groups. As the needs of primary and secondary students differ greatly, we are going to look at these separately. In the appendices section, we have a suggested primary and secondary level template, but we also have a complete example for a 10 year old boy, and a year 11 student (See Appendices G, H, I and J). These plans are called Individual Learning Plans, Individual Education Plans, or Learning Intervention Plans.[4]

Often, to get me thinking about a particular student, I will start with the template *Make the Learning Journey Explicit* (see Appendix K). One of the key things we want to achieve is explicit teaching. Starting to think about accommodations, strategies, scaffolding, repetition and overlearning is an important part of the process to raising achievement in at-risk students.

Making the Learning Journey Explicit (Appendix K) is a great way of starting to think about a student you have identified who needs more. Select a student you currently work with who needs more.

Record their barriers to learning.

What have I noticed that needs adjusting?

What can I do differently?

What accommodations can I put in?

Which programmes, strategies and scaffolding can I use?

How can I give repetition and rehearsal?

The primary level template for an Individual Learning Plan (Appendix G) has 4 key areas:

- **It starts with achievement objectives. From the diagnostic assessment we will select goals and objectives that are *specific, measurable, realistic, achievable* and have a *time* component, in accordance with SMART goals. I often say that our**

expectations for children with learning difficulties need to be different. We need to know their strengths and weaknesses very clearly, and then we set our objectives accordingly. The assessment process that we have just been through allows us to know our students well. We can set higher goals in their areas of strength, and realistic goals in their areas of weakness.

- **The second component of the individual learning plan is how the class teacher plans to adapt the programme. What accommodations will be put in place, and what skills, strategies and programmes will be used to achieve the objectives?**

- **The third area addresses how we plan to use teacher aides and support staff to provide targeted repetition and overlearning.**

- **The fourth area looks at key competencies, and which of the competencies are being targeted. In addition to these four areas, we also want to look at how we will utilise effective software programmes to support the student and raise achievement. Many schools use programmes like Maths Buddy,[5] Mathletics,[6] the Learning Staircase,[7] and Literacy Planet,[8] to name a few. Used as a part of a balanced programme, software can enhance achievement even further.**

The last area we will also look at is developing home–school partnerships, and training parents to do home-reading and fun spelling activities, and possibly assist in other areas if needed. As we work through the next chapter and discuss programmes, this will give you the full information you need, to give you the content and confidence to complete Individual Learning Plans.

The Learning Intervention Plan is very much an individual plan, driven by the achievement needs and circumstances of the student (see Appendix I).

This can be referred to alongside the following discussion.

SMART goals are also used for the secondary plan. It can be very helpful to involve the Special Education Needs Co-ordinator (SENCO) in this process. Chances are, as a subject teacher in secondary education, if you find a student with difficulties in your class, it is very likely they are having difficulties in other subjects. Having a SENCO support you with the learning plan means that you can not only address your subject area, but you can ensure the student is supported across the school. If you have a school-wide IEP, you may like to additionally complete one of the other templates to ensure you get any accommodations needed in place, as well as the strategies, resources and programmes you will use to achieve goals.

In this chapter, we have considered the importance of establishing achievable goals, and planning how we will get there. We have looked at the role of accommodations in this process, as well as possible templates we can use to support us with our teaching. The next chapter will focus on programmes to support our learners.

Chapter Eleven

How Do We Adapt and Develop Our Programmes to Meet the Needs of At-Risk Learners?

Implementing differentiated teaching and third wave strategies is a great start to developing any classroom programme. For a busy classroom teacher, it is much easier to implement class-wide changes to your teaching that will benefit everyone, rather than have individual plans and accommodations for identified students each year. A gradual process of intentional reflective change, to enhance the classroom environment, and reflection on teaching practice to better support students, is a very effective way of improving outcomes.

The following list is a good place to start.[1,2,3,4,5] I recommend that you select one approach and implement it, and once you feel you have this running smoothly, select and implement the next. It is not necessary to work through the list sequentially. You may feel that some areas are already strong in your practice. Many points in the list are suited to both primary and secondary students. Teachers often find it best to start with ones that they feel they can implement easily, so change and benefits are rapid.

- **Plan and record multisensory teaching opportunities for all lessons and units.**

- **Consider structure and routines. Are there any areas that can be strengthened to ensure all at-risk learners get the support they need?**

- **Is planning sequential, and does it follow the developmental stages of learning as much as possible? Are students working on their next steps?**

- **Is there a research base in my classroom practice? E.g., teaching executive functioning skills, addressing emotional needs, or focusing on short term and working memory training.**

- **How can I improve diagnostic use of assessment information?**

- **Can repetition and overlearning opportunities in the classroom be enhanced?**

- **Do all lessons/units have a focus on metacognitive strategies? Does planning reflect this? Are teaching strategies explicitly taught, and is there a focus on repetition and overlearning for these?**

- **Differentiated feedback: have I considered the needs of all learner waves? Is there self-evaluation, peer feedback, and explicit written and verbal feedback at the appropriate level for each learner wave? Introduce feedback sandwiches (state a positive, then a next step and then an overall positive comment) or 'two stars and a wish', to ensure at-risk learners are working on next steps, and are not overloaded with feedback.**

- **Wherever possible, choose high interest topics to teach subject skills.**

- **Make the reasons for learning explicit, and relate these to concrete examples or real-life experience.**

- **For students with processing delays, do I:**
  - Allow more time for tasks?
  - Reduce task requirements?
  - Encourage and allow taking home tasks for homework?
  - Monitor the amount of homework these students have?
  - Reduce quantity of work in favour of quality?

- **Eliminate copying from boards for third wave students – give a copy of notes, and set an activity while others do copying. Perhaps a cloze activity (a comprehension reading task with key words missing for the student to replace).**

- **Provide activities for repetition and to increase fluency.**

- **In oral discussions, give students extra time to respond.**

- **Check students' understanding of instructions and task demands.**

- **Teach and review key vocab words – use glossaries.**

- **Avoid digressions and excessive language – few words are best.**

- **Use Advance Organisers (a tool to link previous learning to new learning), provide written and oral instructions.**

- **Teach study skills, e.g., SQ4R method of textbook reading: Survey (skim read), Question (come up with key questions on topic), Read, Reflect, Recite, (W)rite and Review. Also teach this as a study method.**

The list above contains examples of what we would consider best practice, not only for at-risk learners, but for classrooms generally. Our aim here is to make best practice, common practice. When this happens, our at-risk learners will be well supported, and have the structure and guidance they need to raise achievement and improve outcomes.

For most of us, this work will be an ongoing development throughout the year.

Alongside this process, it is necessary to implement additional programmes to support our at-risk learners. As a SENCO, I saw developing school-wide programmes to support literacy and numeracy, and programmes to address underpinning weaknesses, as a key part of my role. A school-wide focus certainly raises achievement across large numbers of students. The organisation I work with offers online mentoring programmes for SENCOs and teachers to assist with developing policy, practice and teaching strategies.[6] If school-wide programmes are not an option, I suggest teachers set them up for their class. Whether you are a SENCO or a classroom teacher, time does not permit us to meet all the needs of all of our students on our own. Spending time establishing and managing class or school-wide programmes, and getting others to assist with the level of repetition and overlearning required, is a very effective way of raising achievement for at-risk student groups.

Much of what I will share with you about programmes in the rest of this chapter is based on my work as a SENCO in a low decile, small school in the Bay of Plenty, and the work we subsequently did across thirty Bay of Plenty schools, as part of an Eastbay REAP contract. Working with Eastbay REAP, we also established an NZQA approved Teacher Aide Training Programme, focused on enhancing literacy and numeracy in underachieving students. This programme ran successfully for ten years, providing extensive training to allow teacher aides and support staff to play an important part in achieving measurable gains in learning for students. Since the completion of this work in 2014, I have spent the last five years working with schools, nation-wide and in Australia, developing and implementing successful programmes to enhance learning.

Your classroom / school-wide assessment will show you where the focus for your programmes should begin. Very often, I find that reading achievement levels are not what they should be, and this is a great place to start. In primary education, we often have children who have low literacy, and may be reading six months to two years below their chronological age. As students get older, the gap between age and achievement becomes even greater. We often have children achieving three or more years below their chronological age. For some children, this does not improve by the time they reach high school. This results in students entering high school, reading anywhere between a 9 to 12 year old level. These students, due to poor reading, have difficulty accessing the curriculum, and will be set up to fail at high school unless we are able to intervene quickly.

Over recent years, there has been much debate over the way in which reading is taught. Increasingly, the support for a phonemic and phonological approach to reading, and a structured literacy approach (particularly in the early years), is growing widely. Fortunately, many educators are now recognising that a whole language approach is failing up to 40% of our readers, and to improve reading outcomes, a change in the way we teach reading for all readers is required.

In New Zealand and internationally, major research – such as The Rose Report 2006,[7] The US National Reading Panel 2000 Report,[8] Massey University Enhancing Learning Outcomes for Beginning Readers,[9] Ken Rowe's Teacher Reading Report and

Recommendations in Australia (2005)[10] – is clearly showing that a phonemic and phonological approach to reading is the approach moving forward.

Children with difficulties need explicit teaching of the letter–sound correspondences in writing.[11] Students with literacy learning difficulties are unable to hear the individual sounds or phonemes in words. Without instruction in phonemic awareness, they are unable to match letters or letter clusters to sounds in words either for writing or reading. Structured Literacy is explicit instruction that teaches children how to match sound to letters and letters to sound. It has a scope and sequence, meaning all the necessary sounds are taught in a systematic and sequential way that allows *orthographic mapping* to occur. A good programme involves specific instruction in phoneme awareness and manipulation, which is an oral activity, but primes/trains/prompts the brain for print (letter–sound correspondence).

Structured Literacy, using a phonological approach, incorporates instruction down to individual sounds, known as phonemes, in words.

Until relatively recently, it was largely specialist teachers, NZ and International Specific Learning Disabilities (SPELD) and Dyslexia organisations who provided a phonemic and phonological approach to teaching reading. It is very pleasing to see that the science of teaching reading, and evidenced-based dyslexia approaches, are being more widely used. An increasing number of schools are adapting the way they teach reading, writing and spelling to improve literacy outcomes.

Ensuring school-wide literacy success, and meeting the needs of at-risk learners, is paramount in enhancing learning outcomes, and I strongly recommend every school embarks on this journey to upskill teachers and meet the needs of underachieving learners.

Whilst it is outside the scope of this book to provide this training, I recently had the privilege of attending a virtual 1-day seminar with David Kilpatrick.[12,13] David has a PhD and is a professor of psychology for the State University of New York College at Cortland. He is a New York State certified school psychologist with 28 years' experience in schools. He has been teaching courses in learning disabilities and educational psychology since 1994. The seminar was hosted by the International Dyslexia Association (IDA), Ontario. David Kilpatrick is recognised as a leading worldwide specialist in this field.

David talked about the stages or levels of phonological skill development:

1) Early phonological awareness – rhyming first sounds (identification and alliteration) and syllable segmentation

2) Basic phonological awareness – phoneme blending and segmentation

3) Advanced phonological awareness, proficiency, automaticity – the unconscious access to phonemes in spoken words.

He also talked about word-reading skill development and what is needed:

1) Letter names and sounds – phonological storage and retrieval

2) Phonic decoding and encoding (spelling)

3) Orthographic mapping – efficient memory for printed words and rapid sight vocabulary expansion.

One of the challenges I have found, working across many schools, is that even if a school has a phonics approach to spelling, that this isn't necessarily transferred to reading and explicit skill teaching,[12] and the use of decodable texts. Even if a school uses a phonemic/phonological approach, the phonics teaching rarely provides the level of skill necessary as outlined by David Kilpatrick above to achieve optimum outcomes.

David Kilpatrick has several books providing training in this important area.[13] David suggests that, when taught well, using this approach should reduce the number of students with reading difficulties to between 5–8%.

Louisa Moats is also a renowned worldwide specialist in this field. Her book, *Speech to Print*, gives further comprehensive training in this area.[14] I recently had the privilege of attending an online workshop with Louisa Moats hosted by The Ontario Branch of the International Dyslexia Association (ONBIDA). There were many key points made in this webinar presentation, but one of the values of Louisa Moats' work is her explanation of the origins of words in the English Language. Having an understanding of how the various languages contribute, and explicitly teaching this, is so important for student success.

Again, it not my intention to teach this work here, but I do recommend the wisdom of Louisa Moats, along with David Kilpatrick, to assist your professional development.

Louisa Moats confirms previous research. In the webinar she talked about:

- **How reading and spelling development are mediated by phonological awareness**
- **How methods that emphasise language structure are more effective than rote methods**
- **How better spelling leads to better writing**
- **How better spelling leads to better vocabulary and better comprehension**

- **How using encoding instruction improves reading and spelling**

- **How everything is connected and should be respected**

- **The value of orthographic mapping**

- **How phonemic awareness is both hearing and the feeling of speech sounds in the mouth**

- **How visual memory relates to knowledge of phonetics – poor sight word learner: poor phonetics.**

From this it reiterated and confirmed for me why integrated reading, writing and spelling taught through a phonological approach, and structured literacy, is critical for maximising achievement for at-risk learners.

In addition to Kilpatrick and Moats, we have our own Australasian specialists in this area, such as Alison Clarke (who designed Spelfabet)[15] and Lyn Stone (of Lifelong Literacy)[16] in Australia, and New Zealand's own Betsy Sewell (designer of Agility with Sound).[17] Betsy can be contacted for professional development and resources, including decodable books. Her focus is with older struggling readers and her professional development is invaluable in this area. She also has the Word Chain Apps that are available in New Zealand and Australia,[18] and are excellent for repetition and overlearning.

Structured Sequential Literacy Programmes aimed at younger readers, available in New Zealand using Decodable Readers, include New Zealand's *Sunshine Decodables* through Sunshine,[19] and Australia's *Maureen Pollard's Little Learners Love Literacy*, available through Liz Kane Literacy.[20]

Series for older struggling readers, such as Phonic Books UK's *Catch-up Readers*, are available through Learning Matters.[21] Like Betsey Sewell, Liz Kane Literacy and Learners Matters provide PD, bridging the gap between evidence-based learning and classroom practice, as well as decodable books.

A new Early Intervention Programme, the Better Start Literacy Approach,[22] delivered through Canterbury University, is being rolled out in 2021.

The *Better Start Literacy Approach* is an integrated classroom literacy programme for Year 0/1 classrooms, to support children's early reading, writing and oral language success. It incorporates vocabulary development, using quality children's story books, structured teaching of critical phonological awareness skills, and letter–sound knowledge through fun, game-based activities that make explicit links to the reading and spelling context. It also utilises structured small group reading sessions using the new Ready to Read – Phonics Plus early readers series. The *Better Start Literacy Approach* follows a phonics scope and sequence that is used in the class and small group reading teaching.

Whilst structured literacy and phonemic awareness are a prerequisite for achievement in at-risk learners, *do not be fooled* into thinking that all you need to do is address the academic/literacy needs and the job will be done. The multi-modal approach, along with the suggestions in this book, are also needed to support those with learning disabilities, difficulties and differences. It is one of the regrets I have as a parent that I found this out too late. Because there is a social, emotional and behavioural component that goes with learning difficulties, and they can also have other underpinning cognitive weaknesses, it is important that *all* these things are addressed together.

I often have people ask about various programmes, asking me if they are suitable. The rule of thumb I use to determine if a programme is suitable or not is whether it meets the seven key excellences. It must be:

1) Multisensory
2) Structured
3) Sequential
4) Evidence / research based
5) Provide repetition and overlearning
6) Use diagnostic evidence
7) Teach metacognitive strategies.

If programmes don't meet all of the criteria, it doesn't necessarily mean they aren't useful programmes. However, they are more likely to suit first and second wave learners, in the same way as many of our current schools-based programmes are. Sometimes programmes can be adapted so these criteria can be met, but it is important when selecting programmes and resources, in order to ensure third wave needs are met, that these criteria are reflected. The programmes I will discuss in the rest of this chapter follow these guidelines. The structured literacy programmes we have just discussed also meet all these criteria.

My interest in reading programmes developed in the late 1990s. I was invited to a meeting at a local school to look at a reading programme that they were having great success with. As the SENCO, my principal sent me along to find out about it, with a view to implementing it in our own school. At the meeting the school said that they had been running the programme for some time, and the average student had improved 18 months to 2 years in reading, after one or two terms on the programme. My initial response was that they were exaggerating, but as they went on to explain the programme, I could see why it was having such good results. The programme was called the Brenda Lofthouse Parent Tutors in Reading Programme.[23] Brenda was a Resource Teacher of Reading in the Wellington, Upper Hutt area, and she later became a Resource Teacher of Literacy. Her programme involved training teacher aides, parents and community volunteers to support at-risk readers. The programme was based on the popular Pause Prompt Praise programme, but she set up an organisational framework to allow schools to have relatively large numbers of students on the programme and have them monitored. As a Resource Teacher of Reading, travelling around many schools, she found the needs were far greater than she could work with on her own. The programme allowed each school to establish and monitor their own programme.

There were three key things that struck me about the programme, and I could see these were the underlying reasons for its success. Firstly, they trained all the teacher aides, parents and community volunteers, who were known as tutors, to do good book introductions. As teachers, we know that a good book introduction sets a reader up for success. It builds on language experience and it develops vocabulary. I could see that if this was part of the programme, it would work well. Secondly, the programme focused on the six effective strategies that good readers use. The tutor's job was to teach and reinforce the strategies, and give students an opportunity to practise them. Through this process, they were moving students from dependent readers to independence, and the focus was on teaching metacognitive strategies. The third part of the programme asks tutors to focus on comprehension. Practicing retelling, and asking lower and higher-level thinking questions, improves children's understanding of what they read.

Suffice to say, I took the programme back to our school, and we implemented it. We also found that students would improve 18 months to 2 years on the programme after one or two terms, and some children improved 3-4 years once they were on the programme for a year. We invited all our parents to train, so that parents could assist better with home-learning and reading books at home, and we invited parents to act as home-school tutors. Due to my knowledge of underpinning weaknesses and phonological problems of at-risk readers, we taught parents about letter–sound knowledge and letter patterns, developing a resource for this. We asked parents to focus on letter–sound/pattern cues as the first strategy, and if students needed further support, to back it up with other whole language strategies. Through this method, we saw incredible growth with at-risk third wave learners.

As part of the SENCO programme at this school, I had SENCO/board funding to identify and support six at-risk learners. Every year I would bring a specialist assessor in to assess students. The board paid a specialist teacher one day a week to teach these students. The specialist assessor used to come and stay for the week to do this work. At the end of one week, he said to me, 'Jenny, there is something funny with these students. They all have learning difficulties, mostly dyslexia. But they are all scoring higher in their reading subtests than what I would expect, given their learning difficulties.' I told him that we had the students on a tutor reading programme, and we had trained the tutors in a phonological approach as a well as a whole language, and we had asked the tutors and parents to use letter–sound/pattern cues first. He said, 'That's it – what you have done is turn a mainstream programme into a third wave programme, and are getting gains with dyslexic students as well.'

As a result of my successes at this school, I left classroom teaching, and began working with schools and organisations developing literacy programmes and supporting at-risk learners with them. We would go on to establish tutor reading and other programmes in around thirty local schools, as part of an Eastbay REAP literacy initiative. Every school that implemented and managed their programmes well, saw the same excellent outcomes from the programme, including several secondary schools.

I now recommend every school I work with to implement an effective tutor reading programme. Using Brenda Lofthouse's programme, with an additional focus on phonological support, achieves excellent results for all learning waves.

It is outside the scope of this book to train you for the programme, but Brenda Lofthouse has an excellent book.[23] It is simple to use, and contains templates and information you will want to use to establish the programme. SENCOs and teachers have limited time, and in-person additional training can sometimes be challenging to access. Raising Achievement has an online Tutor Reading short course available, which provides the training and resources needed to establish a programme in your school or class.[24]

To further enhance my reading programme, an additional resource I use is the 'Key Comprehension' series.[25] This is used to add depth to best practice classroom teaching of reading, and it can also be used to enhance comprehension in tutor programmes.

In 2005, I completed my Postgraduate Qualification in Literacy with Massey University. Keith Greaney shared some information from work they had undertaken in local schools.[26]

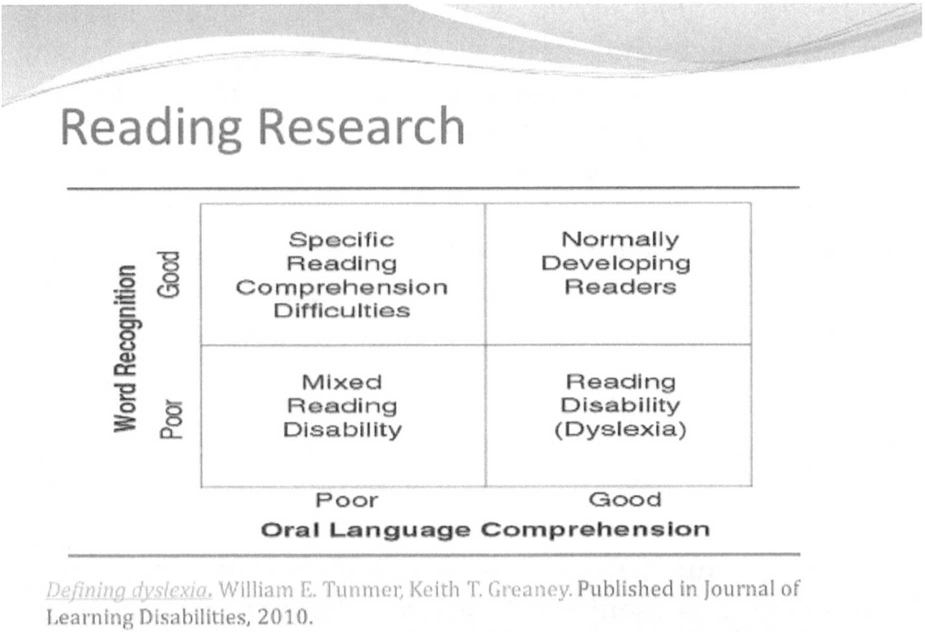

Figure 1. Classification of different categories of reading difficulty according to a model of the proximal causes of reading difficulties. Note: The lines separating the three subtypes of reading difficulty are for representation purposes only, as the two variables that differentiate the subtypes are continuous, not dichotomous.

This figure above shows how students' needs fit into the various quadrants.[26] Some students will decode and comprehend well. A large number are good decoders but poor comprehenders. Some students are poor decoders and comprehenders whilst a smaller percentage of students with dyslexia have good oral/listening comprehension but remain poor decoders. Our job is to identify the needs of our students and ensure the appropriate reading programme is applied.

The authors of *Defining Dyslexia* make the point that the majority of poor readers fall into the *Mixed Ability/Poor Readers* group, all of whom require intensive research-based instruction in phonological-based skills.[26]

In addition, Tunmer and Greaney also make it clear that the dyslexic group (bottom right quadrant) have good oral / listening comprehension of the language. This is not the same as having good reading comprehension. According to their model, this is clearly what differentiates the true dyslexics (probably only about 3% of all poor readers) from the garden variety or mixed ability poor readers, who have the language problem as well as the decoding issues. Even these dyslexic readers still require the phonological-based instruction that the garden variety group require, as their problem in the main, is still poor decoding.

The tutor reading programme assists low literacy and third wave learners to improve decoding and comprehension to raise achievement. The Key Comprehension series resource that we will discuss shortly assists in the building of comprehension skills. With a support programme and this resource, along with best practice classroom teaching, and intensive, research-based instruction in phonological-based skills, we are able to target the needs of all learner groups in reading.

With a structured literacy approach in the junior school, and the use of decodable texts to teach reading instruction, our students will be better equipped to read, write and spell.

The Key Comprehension series resource has been developed by Triune Initiatives Ltd,[25] who also developed the PROBE Reading Comprehension Assessment widely used in schools. If we don't have explicit comprehension teaching, what tends to happen in schools is that we give practise in comprehension through giving students passages to read, and asking questions, but we don't actually teach the skills needed.

The 'Key Comprehension' series resource discusses how developing comprehension skills is a developmental process. When children first learn to read, the focus is on literal or recall questions, where children can go straight back to the text to find the information. The next step is re-organisation of text. Here students are required to link together one or more pieces of information to provide an answer. The next level is inference. Here, readers are asked to look beyond the text, identifying the authors intention and to take meaning from text by clues given. The next level is evaluation, and before you can evaluate, summarise or synthesise ideas in a text, you need to be able to reorganise information and infer. In addition to these skills, readers also need to have the ability to react to text, giving their opinion and backing up their opinion using the text. Having a broad vocabulary also assists comprehension, and the Comprehension series includes a vocabulary focus throughout the resource.

There are three 'Key Comprehension' series resources: Key into Reorganisation, Key into Inference, and Key into Evaluation. Each resource is organised into three independent reading age levels. Children with a reading level of 8 to 10 years, work with level 1. Children reading at 10 to 12 years, work with level 2. Children reading at 12 to 14 years, work with level 3. Teachers select the level they deem appropriate for their students but there is a recommendation that students begin at a lower level than their decoding age. The resource is designed to be an oral language resource, where groups discuss the information given, the questions, and the key words that highlight the answers. In this way, we are modelling how effective thinkers comprehend text, to students who do not yet comprehend well. The texts begin with short one or two sentence texts, progressively moving to paragraphs and half-page texts. They also cover a range of curriculum subjects, so students learn how to carry skills across different settings and subject areas.

Again, it is not my intention to teach the use of the resource here, but to highlight its value and importance as an addition to an effective reading programme. As there is insufficient room to go into these resources in depth, I recommend those who want more information, go to the Triune Initiatives website.[27]

As a SENCO or a classroom teacher, the Brenda Lofthouse Parent Tutors in Reading programme and the 'Key Comprehension' series resource would always be a feature of my school or class reading programme. As shown, the programme and the resource, combined with an effective structured literacy classroom reading programme, meet the needs of all learner types. Through pre-testing, quality intervention and post-testing, significant student gains can be realised and evidenced across all waves of learning.

It is important to develop class or school-wide programmes gradually, ensuring that programmes are implemented thoroughly, and they are effectively improving outcomes. Don't rush through the implementation process. Once one programme is running well, the next can be considered. When I am working with schools to develop policy and practice, I often say that it is a two to five year process to develop a school to a level where they are delivering equity in education and teachers are equipped to meet the needs of at-risk learners, and where evidence of gains in learner outcomes reflects this. Similarly, for a classroom teacher, depending on where they start, one to two years is a realistic time frame to develop programmes and differentiated teaching skills.

The next programme I would often consider is in the area of writing. Brenda Lofthouse has a Parent Tutors in Writing programme that provides excellent results for students whose writing achievement is below expected levels.[28] Again, teacher aides, community volunteers and parents are trained for this role. This programme is run with a group of students rather than individually. The optimum group size is four students, although I have run it with up to six students. It is important that tutors can manage the group easily so that they can focus on writing, otherwise valuable time is lost through group management. The class teacher selects writers who have difficulty with the process of writing and are achieving below their chronological age. The group is often referred to as the Pen Pals Club, but many are now choosing to come up with a personalised name selected by the group.

The writers undertake three to four writing sessions per week with trained tutors. Depending on students' ages, the sessions should run for 30–45 minutes. For high school students, this is often extended to an hour, so students can attend for a whole period rather than coming and going from classes.

Several key aspects of the programme ensure excellent results are achieved. The writers are taught, and practise, brainstorming and mind mapping to generate ideas. A group brainstorm is completed on a topic. In this way, thinking skills are modelled, and students who have difficulty with brainstorming see how others do it. Each student then completes an individual brainstorm using their own ideas. Writers then write using their brainstorm as a plan. Writing does not usually progress past draft form. The focus is on writing a short, quality piece of writing daily. The last part of the session focuses on proofreading and editing, and students are explicitly taught these skills. A focus on strategies that successful writers use is an essential part of the programme. Through repetition and practise, guidance from the tutor, and self-monitoring, many students improve a curriculum level in writing after a term on the programme. Some writers may require longer on the programme to consolidate skills.

Prior to beginning the programme, pre-assessment is undertaken. This involves a ten-minute, unassisted writing sample. A Midland Spelling Scale, and an Alpha to Omega assessment can be used to determine a writer's current level of proficiency and to highlight next steps and writing needs. These assessments are completed again at the end of the term, to reassess achievement and determine next steps. In this way, we are following best practice in terms of pre-assessment, quality intervention and post-assessment. Tutors are trained in programme delivery and essential writing skills. The writing programme assists students to develop writing strategies, and secondary students can build up to a focus on essay writing skills.

For some students, an effective classroom writing programme does not give the repetition and practise that students require to become proficient. A targeted writing programme, like the Brenda Lofthouse Parent Tutors in Writing programme, provides support for these students in a small group setting. The writing sessions can be undertaken during the class writing time, and the tutor can work with their group in the classroom. If desired, the group can be taken at a separate time or in a quiet space outside the classroom.

Again, it is outside the scope of this book to train you in the programme. Brenda Lofthouse's book is simple to use, and contains templates and information you will want to use to establish the programme. Courses are available online to provide training and resources for those interested in establishing a programme in their school or class.[29]

The next programme I would like to consider is the Alpha to Omega Integrated Reading, Writing and Spelling programme.[30] Many of the schools I work with report that their spelling programmes are working well for most students, but there is still a group of students who are underachieving. Schools are now saying that these students show progress quickly once the Alpha to Omega programme is implemented. I have some schools who opt to implement it as a school-wide programme, and other schools that opt to use it only with their underachieving groups.

The programme is very structured and sequential, and it follows the developmental stages in spelling. The programme is divided into three stages. Stage one covers the first 30 letter patterns children need to learn, which should be mastered by 8 years. Stage two covers the next set of letter patterns, which should be mastered by 12 years. Stage three covers the final set of patterns, which should be mastered by 15 years. I use the Alpha to Omega programme with every student I work with, in every class and every school. One of the reasons I value it so highly is that I believe there is a lot to be said for a programme that you can start on entry to school, and carry right throughout the primary school years and into high school. Often children will work with several spelling programmes during their years at school, and this can become confusing, particularly for students with phonological and spelling weaknesses. Students who are more able can go on to stage two and stage three. In this way, each student is working at their level, and students are working and advancing at their own pace. If you have mastered all the stage three patterns, you are a very good speller.

Each student, regardless of age, is assessed on the stage one spelling patterns. Students who have mastered stage one patterns can go on to the stage two assessment, and stage three if necessary. The gaps in their spelling patterns form the starting point for the programme. As a classroom teacher, running the programme class-wide, I group students according to needs and run the programme in the same way I run reading groups. With guided lessons, I utilise independent activities, games and software for repetition and overlearning. One of the reasons the programme is so successful is because it teaches spelling patterns, rather than isolated words. For students who have visual memory problems and difficulty learning sight words, this means that once they learn a particular pattern, they theoretically know all the words with that pattern. The programme uses a multisensory approach, and integrates reading, writing and spelling, so students immediately transfer patterns learned across to their writing. It also provides the amount of repetition and overlearning needed for third wave learners.

As a SENCO, if I have release time from class to allow me to undertake SENCO work, I will identify students in the school who need extra support and run three group sessions weekly. Teacher aides can be trained to work with groups in the classroom, or with withdrawal groups (students who require additional support). The Alpha to Omega text is an excellent manual for showing what to teach, when to teach it and how to teach it. A resource like this is so important for us, as teachers not trained in the phonological approach, and provides valuable information for us to lead our learners to success. Raising Achievement has also developed a phonological online short course programme to provide additional training and resources in this key area.[31]

Raising Achievement has developed letter tiles and dice game resources to support the programme.[32,33] A typical half-hour guided lesson for a teacher, specialist or teacher aide, follows a six-step process for each letter pattern, as follows:

1) The letter pattern is identified, and dictation words are taken from the Alpha to Omega book.

2) Letter tiles are used to make words with the spelling pattern.

3) A dice game, with dice showing all letter patterns taught, is played. In this game, children make, read and spell words. They get two points for words made with the pattern of the day, and one point for other words. This is a great game to reinforce previous letter patterns taught, also. Each time a new pattern is taught, the next dice is added.

4) The Ann Marsh Weird Word Game is played next.[34] This is an excellent game to practise reading and spelling words and non-words. When you focus on non-words, it forces children to use their developing knowledge of letter–sound patterns. It is particularly good for children with underpinning auditory cognitive weaknesses. The game comes with clear instructions. Patterns are colour coded, and there are various stages to suit the level of each student.

5) At this point, you can use any resources you have available in the classroom to reinforce letter patterns. These might include games such as Quiddler (available from Whitcoulls), the Smart Kids games,[35]

and any other spelling programme resources you may have. Raising Achievement offers a CD called Sound Play by Jeannie Cochrane.[36] This CD has 64 printable games and activities. The key here is to have multiple fun ways of undertaking repetition and overlearning.

6) The last step is to read out three dictation sentences, which can be taken from the Alpha to Omega text. Each letter pattern has prepared sentences.

The final, important link to getting this programme running effectively, with excellent outcomes, is to undertake training with parents. We teach parents the letter tiles and dice games. When the letter pattern word lists go home, they are able to support children with the programme they are learning at school. Many parents purchase a set of tiles and a dice game, so they have the resources at home. Some schools are including a set with school stationery at the beginning of the year, so all parents have them. This way, we have the important home-learning link established. A home–school partnership is so important to raising student achievement.

Lower case letters should be used for letter tiles. Written and unwritten sets are available for people who want to save costs.[32] The unwritten sets come with a letter template, so people know what to write on them.

Alpha to Omega is an excellent resource to improve phonological awareness and literacy achievement. As so many of our students with learning difficulties have phonological problems, it is vital that these are addressed, hence the reason I use and recommend this programme so widely.

I would like to discuss two additional programmes before we close this chapter; a junior school language programme and a numeracy programme. The junior school language programme is a preventative programme that sets children up for success.

An effective numeracy programme is also needed for students achieving below their chronological age.

Hei Awhiawhi Tamariki ki te Panui Pukapuka (HPP) is a homegrown New Zealand programme that was developed by Kathryn Atvars while she was working in Special Education, along with Annette Stock – a Speech Language therapist – and Heather Pinfold.[37] It is a research-based programme that had input from the Ministry, and tremendous success when implemented in schools. The programme is based on picture books and teaches early literacy skills. It focuses on developing oral language, rhyme recognition, rhyme creation, onset and rime, and letter–sound knowledge. Parent tutors and teacher aides are trained in the programme, and they work with children one-on-one, three or four times weekly, in a specific way.

I implemented the programme as a SENCO in the low decile school I was in, and I also had the privilege of co-ordinating the programme with five of our local schools. Later on, we applied for Enhanced Programme Funding from Special Education, and put the programme into other schools. The idea is to build students' rich oral vocabulary and to build the literacy skills they are going to need for successful reading and writing. One of the things I value about this programme is that it can be used with children as young as 3 and 4 years of age. By utilising the programme early, it becomes a preventative programme and prepares children for school. So often we wait until a child is six, and then deal with problems that arise.

So many of our programmes are ambulances at the bottom of the cliff, but what could we achieve if we put in place more preventative programmes? Thanks to the research that underpins Hei Awhiawhi Tamariki ki te Panui Pukapuka (HPP), we now know which literacy skills children need to be successful. What if we can set them up before they are 6 years old? HPP is an example of a programme that does exactly this.

The programme has powerful benefits. In one particular school where I was co-ordinator, the school had three years of funding. They came to me and said that all the 5 and 6-year-olds had now been on the programme, and they asked if I would work with the parents of the 4-year-olds that would be coming into school the following year. We trained the parents in the HPP programme, and they worked with their own children at home for the year before they came to school. The school reported that on the school entry test, this group were the highest performing year group that ever entered the school. What's more, they remained the highest performing year group until they left in Year 6. The only intentional difference between year groups was that this group had been through the HPP programme prior to school entry.

Whilst this is only one school's experience, all the schools I have worked with have been able to show considerable achievement gains from this programme, as demonstrated through pre- and post-testing.

The HPP programme has an excellent pre-assessment, which students undertake before beginning the programme. This includes a phonological awareness assessment, the Junior Oral Language Screening test (JOST), a language sample and letter–sound knowledge assessment, and in the case of older students, a running record. At the end of each term, students are reassessed to ascertain gains. Some students only require a term on the programme, while other students may require two or three terms. One of the premises of the programme is that we must put the language in, before we can get the language out. One of the problems we have nationally is that we often have children who are entering school with language levels as low as two and three years. This means that before children are starting school, they are behind the eight ball. Having a programme like HPP is vital if we are going to turn this around, and develop the skills that students need to succeed in school.

As a SENCO, I ran a school-wide HPP programme. If this is not possible in your school, I would consider establishing one in the junior classes, for children who are reading below the age of 7 years. The HPP assessment can be undertaken to highlight the students who will benefit. For students who are 3-4 years old, the JOST test and language sample only is used for assessment. Class teachers are able to train, implement and manage a programme for their own class, if school-wide programmes are not running.

The final programme I would like to discuss is numeracy. Many of our third wave students are also underachieving in this area. Two of the underpinning cognitive weaknesses – short term and working memory, and processing delays – often affect students greatly in mathematics. They also have difficulty learning basic facts, and often have difficulty with processes and procedures for doing tasks. In order to maximise learning, a multisensory approach is needed, with much greater opportunity for repetition and overlearning than what is generally available from the classroom programme alone. Despite some of the shortcomings that have been noted about the success of the numeracy programme, when taught well, the numeracy project programme is an excellent programme for third wave learners.

Firstly, the assessment process determines which stage a child is at, and the concepts needing to be learned at each stage are clearly spelled out, so that achievement is measurable. In this sense, it provides a very structured and sequential programme that sees third wave learners thrive. The teaching methods and activities are multisensory, and equipment is readily available. Third wave students tend to need the equipment much longer than other students. Their journey from concrete to abstract/visualisation takes more time, and for them there seems to be a middle stage, which I call visual. Before they can move to the visualisation stage, they need to be able to see the equipment, but do not need to manipulate it. Students need to have access to materials until they have reached the visualisation stage, and one of the problems, I believe, is that we have removed the equipment too early for many students.

The best way I have found to address the needs of at-risk students is to thoroughly train teachers aides in the numeracy project, and in working with students with learning difficulties. Support staff then take three or four sessions weekly, in addition to classroom programmes. Four to six students in a group is ideal. The groups should be organised based on pre-testing and similar needs. The group can then work at their level on next steps. The programme is planned and monitored closely by the classroom teacher to ensure through pre- and post-testing that accelerated gains are being made.

Raising Achievement offers webinars and online programmes, to support and train teacher aides / support staff in tutor reading, comprehension, tutor writing, Alpha to Omega and numeracy programmes.[38]

Whilst it is fair to say that there isn't the same body of research around numeracy as there is about literacy, it is important to gain an understanding around Mathematics and learning difficulties, if we are to support our children well. A book that I found very helpful, and that answered a lot of questions for me, was a book called *Dyslexia and Mathematics* by T.T. Miles and E. Miles.[39]

For those of you who would like to enhance your maths programmes to better target the needs of all learner groups, this gives you some starting points.

By now you will have realised why I said that enhancing programmes will be a one- to two-year project. You have probably also realised the enormity of this subject, and how teacher training in this area involves much more than one or two days of professional development.

I suggest that you select a target area for programme enhancement, and begin the process. Take one step at a time, implement well, and reach out for guidance as you need to. I hope you enjoy working in this area as much as I have, and gain a great deal of satisfaction in raising student achievement through this process.

Chapter Twelve

How Do We Bring All This Together?

Some of my readers may know that in 2014, I cycled the length of New Zealand. I covered 2140 km in 27 days. Many people, including cyclists and athletes, have said to me, 'How did you achieve such a feat?' They believed that with their own skills and experience, they would not be able to do it.

At the time I was overweight, inexperienced, certainly not an athlete, and in my fifties. The only way to achieve something like this is to 'chunk it'. I remember driving down in the van we had hired from Whakatane to Invercargill. We left early on a Saturday morning, arriving in Invercargill fairly late the following Sunday evening. The whole trip down, I was assessing what I was about to do. The next time I travelled this road would be on a push bike. *Could I make these hills? Would my body hold up? Could I do this?* At times I would find myself panicking, and thinking I was mad to ever think I could achieve such a thing. I fought these fears and blocked them out of my mind. I did complete it, and I completed it by waking up every morning and saying to myself, 'Today my job is to cycle from here to here. It is so many kilometres, and I am sure there is a good coffee shop on the way. I have done this so many times in training. I've got this.' With these thoughts I set off on my way. I didn't think about the next day. I didn't think about the rest of the island, or how long and how hard it was going to be. I only thought of what I had to do that day.

Every days' achievements spurred me on, and before I knew it, I had finished the South Island. In the same way, I finished the North. There is a lot to be said for chunking. By chunking, you can achieve anything. It is my dream that you, the reader, will succeed. You will succeed in becoming a specialist teacher, one who truly meets the needs of at-risk learners, and those who learn differently despite how high the hills are, despite the terrain you come across, and despite the people, training or systems that may appear to stand in your way. We owe it to every child who enters our classroom to give them an experience in education where they can succeed, where they can be prepared for their future, to allow them to take their place in the world and have a fulfilling, happy and bright future. Sadly, this is not yet a reality for a relatively large group of students.

In this chapter, I would like to help you chunk the contents of this book. You are now coming to the end of the book. You have probably thought a lot about what you have read, and how it applies to your teaching and classroom. You may also have completed some of the exercises, and hopefully you are thinking about how you can implement what you have learned. I don't want you to put this book down, thinking, *That was/wasn't a good read*. Rather, I would like the material in this book to assist you in your future, and help you adapt your teaching and skills, so you reach wider learner groups. By now you have an overview of specialist teaching. You have an understanding of the learner types, what their needs are, and some idea of how we are going to meet them. If you are reading this book at the beginning of the school year, you are about to have a brand-new group come into your care. If you are reading this during the year, they are already there. Regardless of how long you have had them, the process will be the same.

I am going to go back through the chapters now, and summarise the key learning points. I will 'chunk' what needs to be done in each chapter to allow you to differentiate your teaching and modify your practice, to ensure you are targeting and enhancing the learning of every student in your class.

Chapter One: What Is the Problem?

- **Understanding learner groups and at-risk students**
- **The four learner waves**
- **The difference between low literacy and third wave students**
- **An overview of underpinning weaknesses.**

Task: Absorb and understand the information.

Chapter Two: What Does an At-Risk Learner Look Like?

- **Identifying at-risk learners**
- **Using the checklist of 32 characteristics (see Appendix A).**

Task: Complete a checklist of the 32 characteristics on all the students in your class who have learning differences (see Appendix A).

Chapter Three: What Does It Feel Like to Be an At-Risk Learner?

- **Understanding reading difficulties**
- **Understanding left–right brain confusion, and how it relates to classroom learning**
- **The implications of learning difficulties and their effect on students.**

Tasks: Complete the reading task, (see Appendix B) and the star and mirrors activity (see Appendix C). Watch Elliott de Neve YouTube clip.[1]

Chapter Four: What Difference Will Teaching for Diversity Make?

- **The work of the Dyslexia Foundation NZ, and of Neil MacKay – British dyslexia specialist**
- **Understanding NEGS and NAGS, and their implications for this area of teaching**
- **The expectations of the United Nations**
- **Understanding strengths and weaknesses – the deficit model as opposed to the strengths model**
- **Making good use of limited funding.**

Task: Absorb and understand the information.

Chapter Five: What Is an Inclusive Model?

- **Inclusion and access to the curriculum**
- **The mandate in NEGS and NAGS of meeting the needs of at-risk students**
- **How the guiding documents support us in this area of education**
- **The seven key excellences in third wave teaching and enhancing learning for all groups.**

Task: Absorb and understand the information.

Chapter Six: Traditional vs. Modern Approaches

- **Martin Westwell – industrial and post-industrial models of education**

- **The importance of effective working memory and executive functioning skills**

- **Barbara Arrowsmith – neuroplasticity, and positive and negative changes in the brain**

- **Neuroscience and the implications for teaching.**

Task: Absorb and understand the information.

Chapter Seven: What Does an Inclusive Classroom Look Like?

- **The learning difficulties continuum**

- **Neil MacKay – Notice and Adjust approach**

- **Creating the necessary learning environment**

- **Implementing strategies and enhancing teaching practice to support at-risk learners.**

Task: Complete the teacher self-review checklist to determine current areas of strength, and areas for development (see Appendix D).

Chapter Eight: Underpinning Cognitive Weaknesses and the Value of Specialist Assessments

- **The important shift in focus to underpinning cognitive weaknesses**

- **Teacher training – developing knowledge and teaching skills to support visual and auditory processing difficulties, short term and working memory, processing delays, phonological weaknesses, and gross and fine motor skills**

- **The value of specialist assessments**
- **The difference between mainstream and third wave programmes.**

Task: Absorb and understand the information.

Chapter Nine: Determining the Next Steps for My Students

- **The complexity of learning waves**
- **Assessment for underpinning cognitive weaknesses**
- **The assessment tools.**

Tasks: Using the Learning Waves Template, tentatively assign your students into appropriate learning waves (see Appendix E).

Prepare your assessment resource kit.

Undertake class-wide screening assessments, and individual assessment on the students you have identified as third wave.

Analyse the assessments and complete an underpinning cognitive weakness template for each student identified (see Appendix F).

Chapter Ten: Accommodations, Strategies and Individual Learning Plans

- **The difference between accommodations and strategies**
- **Moving students from dependence to independence**

- **Targeted accommodations to support underpinning weaknesses**
- **Student planning – making the learning journey explicit**
- **Individual and group education plans – primary and secondary levels.**

Tasks: Using the most appropriate template, design an Individual Learning Plan or IEP/Learning Intervention Plan for each student, using the sample as a guide (see Appendices G, H, I, J).

Using the template in the appendices, complete a Make the Learning Journey Explicit plan for each third wave learner you have identified (see Appendix K).

Chapter Eleven: How Do We Adapt and Develop Our Programmes to Meet the Needs of At-Risk Learners?

- **Making adaptations to teaching practice**
- **The importance of structured literacy**
- **Assessing third wave programmes**
- **Tutor reading and comprehension programmes**
- **Tutor writing programmes**
- **Phonological awareness and Alpha to Omega programme**
- **Oral language programmes**
- **Numeracy programmes.**

Tasks: Select the adaptations you would like to make to your teaching from the list. Choose the one you will begin with, make a plan and implement it.

Select the programmes you would like to implement in your class. Decide on the highest priority programme. Design an implementation process, and carry out implementation.

Chapter Twelve: How Do We Bring All This Together?

- **The importance of 'chunking' to achieve next steps**
- **Chapter summaries and tasks.**

To follow, after this list:

- **Monitoring programmes**
- **Where are we now, and where do we want to be?**
- **Next steps:**
    - Government and Ministry
    - Education Sector
    - Individual Educators.

Task: A commitment to implementation and enhancing teaching practice. The following tasks will need to be completed annually, for each class you take.

1) Complete a 32-characteristic checklist on all the students in your class who have learning differences (see Appendix A).

2) Tentatively assign students to appropriate learning waves (see Appendix E).

3) Undertake class-wide assessment.

4) Complete Underpinning Cognitive Weakness Assessment on identified students.

5) Mark assessment, and complete Class Assessment summary document (see Appendix F).

6) Complete *Make the Learning Journey Explicit* plans (see Appendix K) and Individual Learning Plans (see Appendices G, H, I, J) for all identified students.

7) Implement third wave programmes.

8) Monitor programmes.

9) Maintain an ongoing commitment to developing and implementing new strategies in the list (see chapter eleven) and the teacher self-review checklist (see Appendix D).

Monitoring programmes

Just as we need to differentiate our teaching, our approaches, programmes and feedback, etc., we also have to differentiate our monitoring. Whilst monitoring always differs depending on the age of students, it also has to differ according to waves and learning needs. For example, in junior classes, we will always monitor reading progress and keep running records regularly. However, by the time they get to year 7 and 8, reading progress may be assessed annually with a PAT,[2] e-asTTle,[3] or running record. Provided that a student is reading at or above their chronological age, this is fine, but for students below their chronological age, monitoring needs to occur on a more frequent basis. For third and fourth wave learners, progress needs to be reviewed each term. With all these adaptations to our teaching practice, and support programmes in place, we expect to see accelerated progress. For example, in one term, our goal might be to see six months' gain in reading age. In a year, we might be looking for eighteen months to two years of progress. If expected gains are not being made, we will need to adjust our programmes. For some students, a half-yearly review may be sufficient.

In the past, we have often run reading programmes to suit the year level of the students. In fact, some children need guided reading, extra reading and to take home reading books longer than others. Even students with moderate learning difficulties can take into their teens to read and write close to their chronological age. By about year 7, the formal intensive reading programme at school often stops and we expect students to be reading chapter books (third wave students rarely do). Though differentiated teaching programmes in school need to continue, support programmes should stop when chronological age achievement is reached, not when the average student doesn't need it anymore. Post-testing at the appropriate intervals for each group will form the basis of monitoring, and will also inform next steps. Pre- and post-testing ensures we have measurable and evidenced gains relating to our intervention.

Another concern I have regarding our current system is to do with Special Needs registers. It is great that we have them. I have had the privilege of working with many SENCOs on their registers. One of the things that horrifies me is how long we have gone on tracking failure for some students. They have often been identified as at-risk early on, and have been offered support unsuccessfully, and every year we record their backward slide or minimal achievement. This is *not okay*. Largely, this has occurred because we are attempting to use second wave, mainstream programmes to address third wave problems. The whole aim of this book is to address this problem. I take issue with the word 'Special' in 'Special Needs'. My preference is to call them Learning Needs registers, or Needs registers, rather than 'Special Needs'. When we confuse third and fourth wave learners, as well as low literacy and third wave learners, I believe we are continuing to blur the lines. It creates confusion, and when people don't have clear understanding about varying groups' needs, we don't get the outcomes we want. My speciality area lies with students with learning differences, rather than students with special needs. This is an important distinction. Special Education and specialist teachers largely do a good job with fourth wave learners. It is the third wave learners that are falling through the cracks. This the area we don't have many specialists for.

Where are we now and where do we want to be?

Education is providing for the needs of many students, and providing a platform and environment where they can achieve, and be prepared for successful adult life, and a future in a field of their choosing. However, this is not the case for a relatively large number of students. In this book, we have explored the challenges in education, examined the needs of these students, and considered what changes are needed if we are to provide equity for all student groups, and a level playing field where all can access education to achieve success. Research has provided us with an increasing understanding of brain function, and how optimal learning occurs.[4,5,6,7,8,9] We are now much more aware of brain difference, and are more accepting that people do learn differently. It could be argued that we, up until now, have always offered the best education we could, with the knowledge we have had. To continue with past educational practice in the face of the new knowledge, research, and evidence we have, knowing its negative effects and the poor outcomes it produces for some students, would be negligent. If we are to effectively address the changes that must occur in education, it will take a united approach that sees the government, ministries within governments, the education sector, and all who work in the sector, working together to be responsible to lead and support change.

I read in the 'best evidence synthesis' research that 59% of the difference that can be achieved with students is made at the classroom level.[7] Teachers have the greatest influence. 21% of the difference is attributable to school-level variables and the remaining 20% lies with ministry and government decisions.

As teachers we can begin by changing our practice. We can do this by learning more about the needs of those in at-risk groups in education, by seeking out professional development and by implementing new approaches to meet the needs of those at-risk learners. By focusing on the achievement gains for all student groups, and monitoring and measuring the progress in our classes, we can evidence these gains. You may not be able to change the system and the climate for all students, but you can change and influence the outcomes of the students in your care. When I decided to become a teacher, I did so because I wanted to make a difference in the lives of children. When I did my training, I thought we would be equipped to teach the children in our care. I realised, like many of us have, that we were only equipped to teach 75% of them. This is not fair on us, and it's also not fair for the children who are in the remaining 25% (22% third wave and 3% fourth wave learners). Whilst I recognise that it is frustrating, as well as not fair, and that often we don't have what we need to do the job, I am reminded of the saying, 'It takes a village to raise a child.' As teachers, we are part of that village. Although we need to encourage others to share in this responsibility, and it is vital that we all work together to achieve what needs to be done, we also need to 'be the change we want to see' in education.

I am reminded of a quote by Margaret Mead:

> *Never doubt that a small group of thoughtful,*
> *committed citizens can change the world; indeed,*
> *it's the only thing that ever has.*

To the management and boards of schools, I would say that committing professional development funds and supporting your teachers to develop their practice in this area is one of the most valuable investments you can make. Whilst part of the role of teaching or overseeing the running of a school is to advocate for change at a ministry and government level, it is also to lead the sector with policy, practice, and development to attain excellence *for all* in education. I said earlier in the book that I don't believe that 'the cavalry is coming'. There will never be enough funding allocation and leadership to provide what we need on a plate. In many ways, I feel the sector *is* the cavalry. We can develop policy, practice, and utilise funding in more productive ways to achieve the goals that we so desperately need to achieve.

One of the challenges in education that I believe is holding us back is that we do not have many specialist educators in third wave, at-risk education. At first glance, that statement may sound very strange. We do have specialists, after all. What we do have are specialists, and very good ones, in Special Education. Special Education training is not the same as third wave education training. We also have some excellent people in top jobs, with mainstream, low-literacy teaching excellence and backgrounds in research and best practice. Mainstream education and low-literacy education are not the same as third wave education. We have some very knowledgeable people in the area of gifted and talented students. I repeat, there are few specialists in third wave at-risk education. I further believe that this is why the tail of underachievers in the bell-curve of student achievement in education remains. We have had students who have been through all the good programmes we have, they have worked with our current specialists, and yet they are still achieving well below their chronological age.

I have been working in this field of education for over twenty years. As you know, I chose to become a specialist teacher largely because the education system I was working in was not equipped to meet the needs of my child with dyslexia and ADHD. It took me at least fifteen of those years to become a specialist, and it is only in the last five years that I believe I have sufficient knowledge to call myself an Educational Consultant. What is happening is that we are applying mainstream and Special Education good practice to third wave education, and they are *not* the same thing.

It is my belief that we all, including the ministry and the government, have the best interests of education at heart. I also believe we have done the best job we can with the knowledge skills and resources we have. However, a new field of education is emerging, and it is going to be necessary to develop expertise and resourcing in this evolving area of education, if we are going to make the much-needed changes.

To the ministry and government, I would say that this doesn't have to be an expensive new initiative. Rather, it requires some strategic changes to current systems. What I believe is needed is that the government and Ministry of Education take a more active role in teacher training, and get teachers trained for 100% of the students, not the 75% who are mainstream learners. Recently, the role of Learning Support Co-ordinators/SENCOs has been discussed. Providing specialist training for these people, as specialist third wave educators and leaders, would ensure that there is a trained person in every school. Attaching funded hours to the SENCO role, based on student numbers and even accountability in outcomes, would ensure third wave programmes, rather the mainstream programmes, are applied to at-risk learners. Redirecting the Communities of Learning (COLs) in this way will also consolidate achievement gains. In addition to these strategies, I would also look closely at the credentials of specialist, at-risk educators, and get some of this expertise into the ministry to work alongside current excellent practice in other areas.

Investing in these areas would save countless hours and dollars ensuring the right students get the right programmes. Third wave solutions for third wave learners could stop the funding wastage where we have attempted to apply low literacy programmes to third wave learners unsuccessfully.

When I was on the SPELD National Executive, someone from the ministry said they liked my work because I knew how to take the best of mainstream education and combine it with the best of specialist education. This is exactly what needs to happen here, and it doesn't have to empty the cheque book.

I am excited and passionate about my involvement in creating educational change. To teachers reading this book, you are the heart of education, and I look forward to sharing and hearing about your journey as you enhance your practice to target the needs of all our learners, and improve the outcomes of those at risk. To managers and educational leaders, I am very passionate about my work in schools and in the sector, developing policy and practice to strive for greater excellence in all areas of education.

I trust the contents of this book, and the resources and appendices, will assist you on own journey towards excellence, and help you create magical classrooms where all your learners feel like they belong.

References

Chapter One

[1] Chapman, J. W., Tunmer, W. E., & Prochnow, J. E. (2000). Early reading-related skills and performance, reading self-concept, and the development of academic self-concept: A longitudinal study. *Journal of educational psychology, 92*(4), 703.

[2] Chapman, J. W., & Tunmer, W. E. (2003). Reading difficulties, reading-related self-perceptions, and strategies for overcoming negative self-beliefs. *Reading & Writing Quarterly, 19*(1), 5-24. https://doi.org/10.1080/10573560308205

[3] Raven, J. (2003). Raven progressive matrices. *Handbook of Nonverbal Assessment* (pp. 223-237). Springer, Boston, MA.

[4] Obaid, M. A. S. (2013). The impact of using multi-sensory approach for teaching students with learning disabilities. *Journal of International Education Research (JIER), 9*(1), 75-82.

[5] van Staden, A., & Purcell, N. (2016). Multi-sensory learning strategies to support spelling development: A case study of second-language learners with auditory processing difficulties. *International Journal on Language, Literature and Culture in Education, 3*(1), 40-61.

[6] Blomert, L., & Froyen, D. (2010). Multi-sensory learning and learning to read. *International Journal of Psychophysiology, 77*(3), 195-204.

[7] Shams, L., & Seitz, A. R. (2008). Benefits of multisensory learning. *Trends in Cognitive Sciences, 12*(11), 411-417.

[8] IMSE. (2018, September 24) *What is Orton-Gillingham?* IMSE Journal. Retrieved February 19, 2020, from https://www.orton-gillingham.com/

[9] Dyslexia Foundation of New Zealand. (n.d.) *Recognising dyslexia.* Dyslexia Foundation. Retrieved February 19, 2020, from https://www.dyslexiafoundation.org.nz/info.html

[10] Ministry of Education. (2019, November 4). *Understanding dyslexia*. Inclusive Education. Retrieved February 19, 2020, from https://www.inclusive.tki.org.nz/guides/dyslexia-and-learning/understanding-dyslexia/

[11] Gibbs, J., Appleton, J., & Appleton, R. (2007, June). *Dyspraxia or developmental coordination disorder? Unravelling the enigma*. PMC. Retrieved February 19, 2020, from https://www.ncbi.nlm.nih.gov/pmc/articles/PMC2066137/

[12] Sound Skills. (n.d.) *Auditory processing disorder*. Retrieved February 19, 2020, from https://www.soundskills.co.nz/Auditory%20Processing%20Disorder/Auditory_Processing_Disorder.html

[13] Ministry of Health. (n.d.). *Autism spectrum disorder*. Retrieved February 19, 2020, from https://www.health.govt.nz/your-health/conditions-and-treatments/disabilities/autism-spectrum-disorder

[14] ADHD New Zealand. (n.d.) *ADHD is more common than you think*. Retrieved February 19, 2020, from https://www.adhd.org.nz/adhd-is-more-common-than-you-think.html

[15] Elnakib, A., Soliman, A., Nitzken, M., Casanova, M. F., Gimel'farb, G., & El-Baz, A. (2014). Magnetic resonance imaging findings for dyslexia: A review. *Journal of Biomedical Nanotechnology, 10*(10), 2778-2805.

[16] Goldstand, S., Koslowe, K. C., & Parush, S. (2005). Vision, visual-information processing, and academic performance among seventh-grade schoolchildren: A more significant relationship than we thought? *American Journal of Occupational Therapy, 59*(4), 377-389.

[17] Grisham, D., Powers, M., & Riles, P. (2007). Visual skills of poor readers in high school. *Optometry-Journal of the American Optometric Association, 78*(10), 542-549.

[18] American Academy of Optometry. (n.d.). *Clearer vision for education: Preliminary results*. Retrieved February 19, 2020, from https://www.aaopt.org/detail/knowledge-base-article/clearer-vision-education-preliminary-results

[19] Yalçınkaya, F., & Keith, R. (2008). Understanding auditory processing disorders. *The Turkish Journal of Pediatrics, 50*(2), 101-5.

[20] Moore, D. R. (2006). Auditory processing disorder (APD): Definition, diagnosis, neural basis, and intervention. *Audiological Medicine, 4*(1), 4-11.

[21] Iliadou, V., Bamiou, D. E., Kaprinis, S., Kandylis, D., & Kaprinis, G. (2009). Auditory processing disorders in children suspected of learning disabilities—A need for screening? *International Journal of Pediatric Otorhinolaryngology, 73*(7), 1029-1034.

[22] Anstice, J. (1999). *Clearer vision for education: Preliminary results [abstract]*. Retrieved February 20, 2020, from https://www.aaopt.org/detail/knowledge-base-article/clearer-vision-education-preliminary-results

[23] Maehler, C., & Schuchardt, K. (2011). Working memory in children with learning disabilities: Rethinking the criterion of discrepancy. *International Journal of Disability, Development and Education, 58*(1), 5-17.

[24] Holmes, J. (2012). Working memory and learning difficulties. *Dyslexia Review, 23*(2), 7-10.

[25] Gupta, P., & Sharma, V. (2017). Working memory and learning disabilities: A review. *International Journal of Indian Psychology, 4*(4), 111-121.

[26] Chapman, J. W., Arrow, A. W., Braid, C., Tunmer, W. E., & Greaney, K. T. (2018). *The early literacy project: Final milestone report*. College of Humanities and Social Sciences, Massey University.

[27] Rowe, K. (2005). *Teaching reading: Report and recommendations*. Retrieved February 15, 2021, from https://research.acer.edu.au/tll_misc/5/

[28] Hempenstall, K., & Buckingham, J. (2016). *Read about it: Scientific evidence for effective teaching of reading*. Centre for Independent Studies Limited.

[29] Arrow, A. W. (2010). Emergent literacy skills in New Zealand kindergarten children: Implications for teaching and learning in ECE settings. *He Kupu, 2*(3), 57-69.

[30] Alton-Lee, A. (2003). *Quality teaching for diverse students in schooling: Best evidence synthesis*. Wellington, New Zealand: Ministry of Education Te Tahuhu O Te Matauranga.

[31] Kilpatrick, D. A. (2020, August 20). *The Nature of Reading Development and Difficulties: Implications for Assessment Instruction and Intervention* [Webinar]. IDA Ontario.

Chapter Two

[1] Houghton C. (2015). Under Achievement of Maori and Pasifika Learners and culturally responsive assessment. *Journal of Teacher Inquiry, 1,* 10–12.

[2] Admin, K. S. W. (2016, November 27). *Crossing the body's midline.* Retrieved February 19, 2020, from https://childdevelopment.com.au/areas-of-concern/fine-motor-skills/crossing-the-bodys-midline/

[3] Gieysztor, E. Z., Choińska, A. M., & Paprocka-Borowicz, M. (2018). Persistence of primitive reflexes and associated motor problems in healthy preschool children. *Archives of Medical Science: AMS, 14*(1), 167–173.

Chapter Three

[1] Johnson, S. B., Blum, R. W., & Giedd, J. N. (2009). Adolescent maturity and the brain: the promise and pitfalls of neuroscience research in adolescent health policy. *Journal of Adolescent Health, 45*(3), 216-221.

[2] de Neve, E. (2010, May 29). Dyslexia: *The world the way I see it (Award winning documentary).* Retrieved 19, March 2020, from https://www.youtube.com/watch?v=rhygmurIgG0&feature=youtu.be/

[3] Dharan, V., Meyer, L., & Mincher, N. (2012). At the receiving end: Are policies and practices working to keep students in high schools? *New Zealand Annual Review of Education, 21,* 119-141.

[4] Alton-Lee, A. (2003). *Quality teaching for diverse students in schooling: Best evidence synthesis.* Wellington, New Zealand: Ministry of Education Te Tahuhu O Te Matauranga.

[5] Westwell, M. (2013, August 5). *Session A – When the educational neuroscience meets the Australian curriculum: a strategic approach to teaching and learning* [Paper presentation]. How the brain learns: What lessons are there for teaching? Acer Research Conference 2013, Melbourne.

Chapter Four

[1] Alton-Lee, A. (2003). *Quality teaching for diverse students in schooling: Best evidence synthesis.* Wellington, New Zealand: Ministry of Education Te Tahuhu O Te Matauranga.

[2] 4D. (n.d.). *About Neil Mackay.* Retrieved February 19, 2020, from http://www.4d.org.nz/edge/about_neilmackay.html

[3] Sagi, Y., Tavor, I., Hofstetter, S., Tzur-Moryosef, S., Blumenfeld-Katzir, T., & Assaf, Y. (2012). Learning in the fast lane: New insights into neuroplasticity. *Neuron, 73*(6), 1195-1203.

[4] Education in New Zealand. (2019, June 7). *The National Administration Guidelines (NAGs).* Retrieved February 19, 2020, from https://www.education.govt.nz/our-work/legislation/nags/

[5] Education in New Zealand. (2019, August 30). *The National Education Goals (NEGs).* Retrieved February 19, 2020, from https://www.education.govt.nz/our-work/legislation/negs/

[6] UN News. (2016, September 1). *Inclusive education vital for all, including persons with disabilities – UN rights experts.* Retrieved February 19, 2020, from https://news.un.org/en/story/2016/09/537952-inclusive-education-vital-all-including-persons-disabilities-un-rights-experts

[7] Dyslexia Foundation of NZ. (n.d.). *Our members.* Retrieved February 28, 2020, from http://www.dyslexiafoundation.org.nz/members.html

[8] Alton-Lee, A. (2003). *Quality teaching for diverse students in schooling: Best evidence synthesis.* Wellington, New Zealand: Ministry of Education Te Tahuhu O Te Matauranga.

[9] Elnakib, A., Soliman, A., Nitzken, M., Casanova, M. F., Gimel'farb, G., & El-Baz, A. (2014). Magnetic resonance imaging findings for dyslexia: A review. *Journal of Biomedical Nanotechnology, 10*(10), 2778-2805.

[10] Lopez, S. J., & Louis, M. C. (2009). The principles of strengths-based education. *Journal of College and Character, 10*(4).

[11] Sharples, J., Blatchford, P., & Webster, R. (2016). *Making best use of teaching assistants: Guidance report.* Education Endowment Foundation.

Chapter Five

[1] McBride, H. E. A., & Siegel, L. S. (1997). Learning disabilities and adolescent suicide. *Journal of Learning Disabilities, 30*(6), 652-659.

[2] Harlow, C. W. (2003). *Education and correctional populations*. Bureau of Justice Statistics Special Report. U.S. Department of Justice.

[3] Westwell, M. (2013, August 5). *Session A – When the educational neuroscience meets the Australian curriculum: a strategic approach to teaching and learning* [Paper presentation]. How the brain learns: What lessons are there for teaching? Acer Research Conference 2013, Melbourne.

[4] Dharan, V., Meyer, L., & Mincher, N. (2012). At the receiving end: Are policies and practices working to keep students in high schools? *New Zealand Annual Review of Education, 21*, 119-141.

[5] Linares-Orama, N. (2005). Language-learning disorders and youth incarceration. *Journal of Communication Disorders, 38*(4), 311-319.

[6] Silva, P. A. (1990). The Dunedin multidisciplinary health and development study: A 15-year longitudinal study. *Paediatric and Perinatal Epidemiology, 4*(1), 76-107.

[7] Education in New Zealand. (2019, August 30). *The National Education Goals (NEGs)*. Retrieved February 19, 2020, from https://www.education.govt.nz/our-work/legislation/negs/

[8] Education in New Zealand. (2019, June 7). *The National Administration Guidelines (NAGs)*. Retrieved February 19, 2020, from https://www.education.govt.nz/our-work/legislation/nags/

[9] The New Zealand Curriculum. (n.d.). *The New Zealand Curriculum*. Retrieved February 19, 2020, from http://nzcurriculum.tki.org.nz/The-New-Zealand-Curriculum

[10] Harrington-Atkinson, T. (2017, October 18). *Fleming VARK Theory*. Retrieved February 19, 2020, from https://tracyharringtonatkinson.com/fleming-vark-theory/

[11] Obaid, M. A. S. (2013). The impact of using multi-sensory approach for teaching students with learning disabilities. *Journal of International Education Research (JIER), 9*(1), 75-82.

[12] van Staden, A., & Purcell, N. (2016). Multi-sensory learning strategies to support spelling development: A case study of second-

language learners with auditory processing difficulties. *International Journal on Language, Literature and Culture in Education, 3*(1), 40-61.

[13] Blomert, L., & Froyen, D. (2010). Multi-sensory learning and learning to read. *International Journal of Psychophysiology, 77*(3), 195-204.

[14] Shams, L., & Seitz, A. R. (2008). Benefits of multisensory learning. *Trends in Cognitive Sciences, 12*(11), 411-417.

[15] IMSE. (2018, September 24) *What is Orton-Gillingham?* IMSE Journal. Retrieved February 19, 2020, from https://www.orton-gillingham.com/

[16] Shams, L., & Seitz, A. R. (2008). Benefits of multisensory learning. *Trends in Cognitive Sciences, 12*(11), 411-417.

[17] Ministry of Education. (2008). *Book 2: The Diagnostic Interview, Numeracy professional development projects*. Ministry of Education.

[18] Hornsby, B., Shear, F., & Pool, J. (2006). *Alpha to Omega: The A–Z of teaching reading, writing and spelling, 6th edition*. Heinemann.

[19] Pekrun, R. (2011). Emotions as drivers of learning and cognitive development. *New Perspectives on Affect and Learning Technologies* (pp. 23-39). Springer, New York, NY.

[20] Tyng, C. M., Amin, H. U., Saad, M. N., & Malik, A. S. (2017). The influences of emotion on learning and memory. *Frontiers in Psychology, 8*, 1454.

[21] Malekpour, M., Aghababaei, S., & Abedi, A. (2013). Working memory and learning disabilities. *International Journal of Developmental Disabilities, 59*(1), 35-46.

[22] Holmes, J. (2012). Working memory and learning difficulties. *Dyslexia Review, 23*(2), 7-10.

[23] Bull, R., Espy, K. A., & Wiebe, S. A. (2008). Short-term memory, working memory, and executive functioning in preschoolers: Longitudinal predictors of mathematical achievement at age 7 years. *Developmental Neuropsychology, 33*(3), 205-228.

[24] Silva, P. A. (1990). The Dunedin multidisciplinary health and development study: A 15 year longitudinal study. *Paediatric and Perinatal Epidemiology, 4*(1), 76-107.

[25] Westwell, M. (2013, August 5). *Session A – When the educational neuroscience meets the Australian curriculum: a strategic approach to teaching and learning* [Paper presentation]. How the brain learns: What lessons are there for teaching? Acer Research Conference 2013, Melbourne.

[26] Kang, S. H. (2016). Spaced repetition promotes efficient and effective learning: Policy implications for instruction. *Policy Insights from the Behavioral and Brain Sciences, 3*(1), 12-19.

[27] Driskell, J. E., Willis, R. P., & Copper, C. (1992). Effect of overlearning on retention. *Journal of Applied Psychology, 77*(5), 615.

[28] White, D. (2013, August 5). *Session D – A pedagogical decalogue: discerning the practical implications of brain-based learning research on pedagogical practice in Catholic schools* [Paper presentation]. How the brain learns: What lessons are there for teaching? Acer Research Conference 2013, Melbourne.

[29] Maths Buddy. (n.d.). *New Zealand's #1 Online Maths Teacher*. Retrieved March 29, 2020, from https://www.mathsbuddy.co.nz/

[30] Mathletics USA. (2020, March 24). *Mathletics USA: Empowering math learning online*. Retrieved March 29, 2020, from https://www.mathletics.com/

[31] Literacy Planet. (n.d.). *Making learning fun*. Retrieved from https://www.literacyplanet.com/au/

[32] The Learning Staircase. (n.d.). *The learning staircase*. Retrieved March 29, 2020, from https://learningstaircase.co.nz/

[33] Jungle Memory. (n.d.). *Jungle memory*. Retrieved March 29, 2020, from https://junglememory.com/

[34] Luminosity. (n.d.). *Lumosity brain training: Challenge & improve your mind*. Retrieved March 29, 2020, from https://www.lumosity.com/en/

[35] Sewell, B. (2017). *Wordchain is part of agility with sound*. Retrieved March 14, 2021, from https://wordchain.co.nz/

Chapter Six

[1] Westwell, M. (2013, August 5). *Session A – When the educational neuroscience meets the Australian curriculum: a strategic approach to teaching and learning* [Paper presentation]. How the brain learns: What lessons are there for teaching? Acer Research Conference 2013, Melbourne.

[2] Reigeluth, C. M. (2011). An instructional theory for the post-industrial age. *Educational Technology, 51*(5), 25-29.

[3] Silva, P. A. (1990). The Dunedin multidisciplinary health and development study: A 15 year longitudinal study. *Paediatric and Perinatal Epidemiology, 4*(1), 76-107.

[4] Cragg, L., & Gilmore, C. (2014, January 9). *Skills underlying mathematics: The role of executive function in the development of mathematics proficiency*. Science Direct. Retrieved February 20, 2020, from https://www.sciencedirect.com/science/article/pii/S2211949313000422

[5] Arrowsmith-Young, B. (2013). *The woman who changed her brain: How I left my learning disability behind and other stories of cognitive transformation*. Simon and Schuster.

[6] Scaddan, M. (2009). *40 Engaging Brain Based Tools for the Classroom.* Corwin Press.

[7] Howard-Jones, P. (2013, August 6). *Plenary 3 – Minds, brains and learning games* [Paper presentation]. How the brain learns: What lessons are there for teaching? Acer Research Conference 2013, Melbourne.

[8] The Education Hub. (2019, December 5). *How to integrate effective feedback into your classroom.* Retrieved February 20, 2020, from https://theeducationhub.org.nz/how-to-integrate-effective-feedback-into-your-classroom/

[9] Waldie, K. E., Austin, J., Hattie, J. A., & Fairbrass, M. (2014). SPELD NZ remedial intervention for dyslexia. *New Zealand Journal of Educational Studies, 49*(1), 21.

[10] Moreau, D., Kirk, I. J., & Waldie, K. E. (2017). High-intensity training enhances executive function in children in a randomized, placebo-controlled trial. *Elife, 6*, e25062.

[11] MovinCog. (n.d.). *MovinCog*. Retrieved March 14, 2020, from https://movincog.wixsite.com/movincog

Chapter Seven

[1] Dyslexia Foundation of New Zealand. (n.d.) *Recognising dyslexia*. Dyslexia Foundation. Retrieved February 19, 2020, from https://www.dyslexiafoundation.org.nz/info.html

[2] Ministry of Education. (2019, November 4). *Dyslexia and Learning*. Inclusive Education. Retrieved February 19, 2020, from https://www.inclusive.tki.org.nz/guides/dyslexia-and-learning/#understand

[3] Gibbs, J., Appleton, J., & Appleton, R. (2007, June). *Dyspraxia or developmental coordination disorder? Unravelling the enigma*. PMC. Retrieved February 19, 2020, from https://www.ncbi.nlm.nih.gov/pmc/articles/PMC2066137/

[4] Sound Skills. (n.d.) *Auditory processing disorder*. Retrieved February 19, 2020, from https://www.soundskills.co.nz/Auditory%20Processing%20Disorder/Auditory_Processing_Disorder.html

[5] Esplin, J., & Wright, C. (2014). *Auditory processing disorder: New Zealand review*. Wellington, New Zealand: Sapere Research Group.

[6] Ministry of Health. (n.d.). *Autism spectrum disorder*. Retrieved February 19, 2020, from https://www.health.govt.nz/your-health/conditions-and-treatments/disabilities/autism-spectrum-disorder

[7] ADHD New Zealand. (n.d.) *ADHD is more common than you think*. Retrieved February 19, 2020, from https://www.adhd.org.nz/adhd-is-more-common-than-you-think.html

[8] Schumacher, J., Hoffmann, P., Schmäl, C., Schulte-Körne, G., & Nöthen, M. M. (2007). Genetics of dyslexia: The evolving landscape. *Journal of Medical Genetics, 44*(5), 289-297.

[9] Elnakib, A., Soliman, A., Nitzken, M., Casanova, M. F., Gimel'farb, G., & El-Baz, A. (2014). Magnetic resonance imaging findings for dyslexia: A review. *Journal of Biomedical Nanotechnology, 10*(10), 2778-2805.

[10] Hudson, R. F., High, L., & Otaiba, S. A. (2007). Dyslexia and the brain: What does current research tell us? *The Reading Teacher, 60*(6), 506-515.

[11] Davis, R. D., & Braun, E. M. (2011). *The gift of dyslexia: why some of the brightest people can't read and how they can learn*. Souvenir Press.

[12] Dyslexia Foundation. (n.d.). *Notice and Adjust*. Retrieved February 20, 2020, from http://www.dyslexiafoundation.org.nz/neil_mackays.html

[13] The New Zealand Curriculum. (n.d.). *The New Zealand Curriculum*. Retrieved February 19, 2020, from http://nzcurriculum.tki.org.nz/The-New-Zealand-Curriculum

[14] Education in New Zealand. (2019, August 30). *The National Education Goals (NEGs)*. Retrieved February 19, 2020, from https://www.education.govt.nz/our-work/legislation/negs

[15] Guy R, & Byrne, B. (2013). Article commentary: Neuroscience and learning: Implications for teaching practice. *Journal of Experimental Neuroscience, 7*, 39-42.

[16] Goswami, U. (2008). Principles of learning, implications for teaching: A cognitive neuroscience perspective. *Journal of Philosophy of Education, 42*(3-4), 381-399.

[17] Osborne, M. (2016). Innovative learning environments. *CORE Education White paper*.

[18] Alansari, M. (2018, May 17). *Modern classrooms won't fix education*. Retrieved February 20, 2020, from https://www.auckland.ac.nz/en/news/2018/05/17/modern-classrooms-wont-fix-education.html

[19] Tony Buzan Mind Mapping. (n.d.). *Tony Buzan Mind Mapping Course*. Retrieved February 20, 2020, from https://www.tonybuzan.edu.sg/course/tony-buzan-mind-mapping/

[20] Triune Initiatives. (n.d.). *KEY comprehension series*. Retrieved February 20, 2020, from https://comprehenz.com/resources-all-resources/resources-teaching/key-comp-series/

[21] Proctor, R. (2020) Cover Image. *Journal of Ideas* (personal journal). Reproduced with permission.

[22] Scaddan, M. A. (2008). *40 engaging brain-based tools for the classroom*. Corwin Press.

Chapter Eight

[1] Goldstand, S., Koslowe, K. C., & Parush, S. (2005). Vision, visual-information processing, and academic performance among seventh-grade schoolchildren: A more significant relationship than we thought? *American Journal of Occupational Therapy, 59*(4), 377-389.

[2] Grisham, D., Powers, M., & Riles, P. (2007). Visual skills of poor readers in high school. *Optometry-Journal of the American Optometric Association, 78*(10), 542-549.

[3] Anstice, J. (1999). *Clearer vision for education: Preliminary results [abstract]*. Retrieved February 20, 2020, from https://www.aaopt.org/detail/knowledge-base-article/clearer-vision-education-preliminary-results

[4] Shin, H. S., Park, S. C., & Park, C. M. (2009). Relationship between accommodative and vergence dysfunctions and academic achievement for primary school children. *Ophthalmic and Physiological Optics, 29*(6), 615-624.

[5] Warren, S. (n.d.). *Home*. Retrieved May 27, 2020, from http://www.icept.co.nz/

[6] Admin, K. S. W. (2016, November 27). *Crossing the body's midline*. Retrieved February 19, 2020, from https://childdevelopment.com.au/areas-of-concern/fine-motor-skills/crossing-the-bodys-midline/

[7] Psychological Assessments Australia (n.d.). *Woodcock Johnson fourth edition – Australasian adaptation archives*. Retrieved May 27, 2020, from https://paa.com.au/product/wj-iv/

[8] Waldie, K. E., Austin, J., Hattie, J. A., & Fairbrass, M. (2014). SPELD NZ remedial intervention for dyslexia. *New Zealand Journal of Educational Studies, 49*(1), 21.

Chapter Nine

[1] Wormald, C. (2020, January 29). *Intellectually gifted students often have learning disabilities*. Retrieved February 20, 2020, from https://theconversation.com/intellectually-gifted-students-often-have-learning-disabilities-37276

[2] Raising Achievement. (n.d.). *Raising Achievement*. Retrieved February 20, 2020, from http://www.raisingachievement.co.nz/

[3] Hornsby, B., Shear, F., & Pool, J. (2006). *Alpha to Omega: The A–Z of teaching reading, writing and spelling, 6th edition*. Heinemann.

[4] Parkin, C., Pool, B., & Parkin, C. (2002). *PROBE: Reading assessment: With an emphasis on high-level comprehension*. Triune Initiatives.

[5] Ministry of Education. (2008). Book 2: *The diagnostic interview, Numeracy professional development projects*. Ministry of Education.

[6] Ministry of Education: Te Tahuhu O Te Matauranga. (n.d.). *Student support: Hei awhiawhi tamariki ki te panui pukapuka (HPP)*. Retrieved February 20, 2020, from https://literacyonline.tki.org.nz/Literacy-Online/Planning-for-my-students-needs/Resources-research-and-professional-support/Student-support

[7] Croft, C. (2001, May). *Resource bank in English for school-based assessment* [Paper presentation]. 27th annual conference of the International Association for Educational Assessment (IAEA), Rio de Janeiro. Retrieved February 15, 2021, from https://www.nzcer.org.nz/system/files/10376.pdf

[8] NZ Maths. (n.d.). *Book 2: The Diagnostic Interview*. Retrieved December 6, 2020, from https://nzmaths.co.nz/sites/default/files/Numeracy/2008numPDFs/NumBk2.pdf

[9] NZ Maths. (n, d). *GloSS*. Retrieved March 29, 2020, from https://nzmaths.co.nz/gloss-forms

[10] NZ Maths. (n.d.). *Junior assessment of mathematics*. Retrieved March 29, 2020, from https://nzmaths.co.nz/junior-assessment-mathematics

Chapter Ten

[1] Ministry of Education: *Te Tahuhu O Te Matauranga. (n.d.). Student support: Hei awhiawhi tamariki ki te panui pukapuka (HPP)*. Retrieved February 20, 2020, from https://literacyonline.tki.org.nz/Literacy-Online/Planning-for-my-students-needs/Resources-research-and-professional-support/Student-support

[2] Moving Smart. (n.d.). *Perceptual motor program*. Retrieved December 6, 2020, from https://www.movingsmart.co.nz

[3] Mackay, N. *Supporting Writing with Highlighted Lines*. Reproduced with permission.

[4] Parents.education.govt.nz. (2020, February 17). *Individual plans (IPs) and individual education plans (IEPs)*. Retrieved May 28, 2020, from https://parents.education.govt.nz/learning-support/learning-support-needs/individual-plans-ips-and-individual-education-plans-ieps/

[5] Maths Buddy. (n.d.). *New Zealand's #1 online maths teacher*. Retrieved March 29, 2020, from https://www.mathsbuddy.co.nz/

[6] Mathletics USA. (2020, March 24). *Mathletics USA: Empowering math learning online*. Retrieved March 29, 2020, from https://www.mathletics.com/

[7] The Learning Staircase. (n.d.). *The learning staircase*. Retrieved March 29, 2020, from https://learningstaircase.co.nz/

[8] Literacy Planet. (n.d.). *Making learning fun*. Retrieved from https://www.literacyplanet.com/au/

Chapter Eleven

[1] MacKay, N. (2008). *Removing dyslexia as a barrier to achievement: The dyslexia friendly schools toolkit*. SEN Marketing.

[2] Dyslexia Foundation of New Zealand. (n.d.). *Dyslexia foundation of New Zealand*. Retrieved February 20, 2020, from https://www.dyslexiafoundation.org.nz/

[3] White, D. (2013, August 5). *Session D – A pedagogical decalogue: discerning the practical implications of brain-based learning research on pedagogical practice in Catholic schools* [Paper presentation]. How the brain learns: What lessons are there for teaching? Acer Research Conference 2013, Melbourne.

[4] Scaddan, M. (2009). *40 Engaging Brain Based Tools for the Classroom*. Corwin Press.

[5] SPELD New Zealand. (2019, October 16). *Dyslexia and other learning difficulties*. Retrieved February 20, 2020, from https://www.speld.org.nz/

[6] Raising Achievement. (n.d) *Online courses*. Retrieved February 20,2020, from https://raisingachievement.co.nz/online-courses/

[7] Rose, J. (2006). *Independent review of the teaching of early reading: Final report*. London: Department of Education and Skills.

[8] National Reading Panel (US), National Institute of Child Health, & Human Development (US). (2000). *Teaching children to read: An evidence-based assessment of the scientific research literature on reading and its implications for reading instruction: Reports of the subgroups*. National Institute of Child Health and Human Development, National Institutes of Health.

[9] Chapman, J. W., Arrow, A. W., Braid, C., Tunmer, W. E., & Greaney, K. T. (2018). *The Early Literacy Project: Final milestone report*. Massey University.

[10] Rowe, K., & National Inquiry into the Teaching of Literacy (Australia). (2005). *Teaching Reading: Report and Recommendations*. Department of Education, Science and Training. Retrieved February 16, 2021, from https://research.acer.edu.au/tll_misc/5

[11] Archer, A. (2019, April 19) *Why Explicit Instruction?* Retrieved February 15, 2021, from https://www.youtube.com/watch?v=i-qNpFtcynI

[12] Kilpatrick, D. A. (2015). *Essentials of assessing, preventing, and overcoming reading difficulties*. John Wiley & Sons.

[13] Kilpatrick, D. A. (2018). *Equipped for reading success: A comprehensive, step-by-step program for developing phoneme awareness and fluent word recognition*. Casey & Kirsch Publishers.

[14] Moats, L. C. (2020). *Speech to print: Language essentials for teachers* (3rd ed.). Brookes Publishing.

[15] Spelfabet. (n.d.). *Spelfabet*. Retrieved on March 14, 2021, from https://www.spelfabet.com.au/

[16] Stone, L. (n.d.). *Bringing high quality, research-supported literacy instruction to teachers and families*. Lifelong Literacy. Retrieved on March 14, 2021, from https://lifelongliteracy.com/

[17] Agility with Sound. (n.d.). *The complete literacy programme for older students*. Retrieved on March 14, 2021, from https://agilitywithsound.co.nz/

[18] Sewell, B. (2017). *Wordchain is part of agility with sound*. Retrieved March 14, 2021, from https://wordchain.co.nz/

[19] Sunshine Books. (n.d.). *Sunshine Phonics Decodable Books*. Retrieved on March 14, 2021, from https://www.sunshine.co.nz

[20] Liz Kane Literacy. (n.d.). *Welcome to Liz Kane Literacy*. Retrieved on March 14, 2021, from https://lizkaneliteracy.co.nz/

[21] Learning Matters. (n.d.). *Welcome to Learning Matters*. Retrieved on March 14, 2021, from https://www.learningmatters.co.nz

[22] Better Start Literacy Approach. (n.d.). *Literacy approach: Te ara reo matatini*. Retrieved on March 14, 2021, from https://www.betterstartapproach.com/

[23] Lofthouse, B. (1997). *Parent tutors in reading*. Mana Education Centre. Retrieved March 18, 2021, from https://raisingachievement.co.nz/product/parent-tutors-in-reading-brenda-lofthouse/

[24] Raising Achievement. (n.d.). *Online courses*. Retrieved February 20, 2020, from https://raisingachievement.co.nz/online-courses/

[25] Triune Initiatives. (n.d.). *KEY comprehension series*. Retrieved February 20, 2020, from https://comprehenz.com/resources-all-resources/resources-teaching/key-comp-series/

[26] Tunmer, W., Greaney, K. (2009, October 15). Defining Dyslexia. *Journal of Learning Disabilities, 43*(3), 229–243. https://doi.org/10.1177/0022219409345009

[27] Triune Initiatives. (n.d.). *KEY comprehension series*. Retrieved February 20, 2020, from https://comprehenz.com/resources-all-resources/resources-teaching/key-comp-series/

[28] Lofthouse, B. (1997). *Parent tutors in reading*. Mana Education Centre. Retrieved March 18, 2021, from https://raisingachievement.co.nz/product/parent-tutors-in-reading-brenda-lofthouse/

[29] Raising Achievement. (n.d.). *Managing programs for at-risk writers*. Retrieved March 14, 2021, from https://raisingachievement.co.nz/tutor-writing-online-course/

[30] Hornsby, B., Shear, F., & Pool, J. (2006). *Alpha to Omega: The A–Z of teaching reading, writing and spelling, 6th edition*. Heinemann.

[31] Raising Achievement. (n.d.). *Phonological awareness and learning difficulties*. Retrieved March 14, 2021, from https://raisingachievement.co.nz/phonological-awareness-online-course/

[32] Raising Achievement. (n.d.). *Letter tiles – Written*. Retrieved March 14, 2021, from https://raisingachievement.co.nz/product/letter-tiles-written/

[33] Raising Achievement. (n.d.). *Dice game – Written*. Retrieved March 14, 2021, from https://raisingachievement.co.nz/product/dice-game-written/

[34] Raising Achievement. (n.d.). *Weird word game – Anne Marsh*. Retrieved March 14, 2021, from https://raisingachievement.co.nz/product/weird-word-game-anne-marsh/

[35] Smart Kids. (n.d.). *Smart Kids*. Retrieved on March 14, 2021, from https://www.smartkids.co.nz/

[36] Raising Achievement. (n.d.). *Sound play CD – Jeannie Cochrane*. Retrieved March 14, 2021, from https://raisingachievement.co.nz/product/sound-play-cd-jeannie-cochrane/

[37] Ministry of Education: Te Tahuhu O Te Matauranga. (n.d.). *Student support: Hei awhiawhi tamariki ki te panui pukapuka (HPP)*. Retrieved February 20, 2020, from https://literacyonline.tki.org.nz/Literacy-Online/Planning-for-my-students-needs/Resources-research-and-professional-support/Student-support

[38] Raising Achievement. (n.d.). *Online courses*. Retrieved February 20, 2020, from https://raisingachievement.co.nz/online-courses/

[39] Miles, T. R., & Miles, E. (Eds.). (2004). *Dyslexia and mathematics*. Psychology Press.

Chapter Twelve

[1] de Neve, E. (2010, May 29). *Dyslexia: The world the way I see it (Award winning documentary)*. Retrieved 19, March 2020, from https://www.youtube.com/watch?v=rhygmurIgG0&feature=youtu.be/

[2] New Zealand Council for Educational Research. (n.d.). *Progressive achievement tests (PATs)*. Retrieved May 28, 2020, from https://nzcer.org.nz/tests/pats

[3] Electronic Assessment Tools for Teaching and Learning (e-asTTle). (n.d.). *Home*. Retrieved May 28, 2020, from https://e-asttle.tki.org.nz/

[4] Elnakib, A., Soliman, A., Nitzken, M., Casanova, M. F., Gimel'farb, G., & El-Baz, A. (2014). Magnetic resonance imaging findings for dyslexia: A review. *Journal of Biomedical Nanotechnology, 10*(10), 2778-2805.

[5] Westwell, M. (2013, August 5). *Session A – When the educational neuroscience meets the Australian curriculum: a strategic approach to teaching and learning* [Paper presentation]. How the brain learns: What lessons are there for teaching? Acer Research Conference 2013, Melbourne.

[6] Silva, P. A. (1990). The Dunedin multidisciplinary health and development study: A 15 year longitudinal study. *Paediatric and Perinatal Epidemiology*, 4(1), 76-107.

[7] Alton-Lee, A. (2003). *Quality teaching for diverse students in schooling: Best evidence synthesis*. Wellington, New Zealand: Ministry of Education.

[8] Morris, R. J., & Mather, N. (2008). *Evidence-based interventions for students with learning and behavioral challenges*. Routledge.

[9] MacKay, N. (2012). *Removing dyslexia as a barrier to achievement: The dyslexia friendly schools toolkit*. SEN Marketing.

Appendices

Appendix A

Observable Characteristics of Children with Learning Differences

Often:

1) A child who is intelligent but doesn't always perform to intelligence level or expectations.
2) The child who appears to have selective hearing and hears some things but not others.
3) The child who never has what they need at the right time and who forgets everything.
4) The child whose room and desk are always in a mess and who always has a dishevelled appearance.
5) The clumsy child who trips over their own feet.
6) The child who doesn't pick up the rules of socialising – who always interrupts or doesn't look at the person who is speaking to them.
7) A child who reads the sequence of letters wrong and gets confused by the order of numbers.
8) The child who can't keep their hands to themselves and is always touching others.

9) The child who carries on a joke long after it has finished.

10) The child who gets confused between breakfast, lunch and dinner and mixes up yesterday, today and tomorrow, and whose timing is off.

11) The child who gets frustrated when they make a mistake and who goes from 0–100 in terms of anger when something upsets them in a split second.

12) They are often afraid to try new things and are frightened by change in routines.

13) They would rather be thought of as naughty than thought of as stupid, so behave badly to detract from the real issue.

14) This is the child who has difficulty with comprehension. They can't picture things in their mind or remember what they see.

15) This is the child who sits quietly but doesn't learn.

16) These children often have poor sense awareness. They might hug the cat too tightly, press too hard with their pencil, be covered in bruises, and not know how they got them, or wear t-shirts in winter and jerseys in summer.

17) This is an older child whose language often comes out jumbled, they stop and start in the middle of sentences, and they may talk about 'hopsitals', 'aminals' and 'emenies'. They get the sequence of syllables out of order.

18) They are often good strategists but don't get a riddle or a joke.

19) They get bored easily and yawn a lot during learning.

20) They may have unexpected difficulties with some motor skills – be good at playing soccer but trip over their own feet at other times.

21) They have performance inconsistency.

22) They are often very particular and want things done their way.

23) They often tell tales on others which gets them into trouble. They may be bossy at times, or be the bully at other times, and even be the one who is bullied.

24) They often play well with children younger or older than themselves but find it difficult to keep friends of the same age.

25) They often skip or add words when reading aloud, or miss lines.

26) They often see things as black or white and they don't get inference or sarcasm.

27) These children are often thought of as lazy because they are quick to do things they like, but slow when it involves work.

28) This is the child who has confusing or unexpected difficulties. Maybe they can add or multiply but not subtract or divide, they can't do maths in their head but can do it on paper.

29) They often make social mistakes. They smile at everyone, greet strangers with open arms, say hello to everyone they see and have a good nature which leads them into trouble as the 'fall guy'.

30) They often say things seemingly off topic.

31) They sometimes understand complex things but then have trouble doing something others find easy.

32) Occasionally they have a big chip on their shoulder.

These characteristics are useful for parents or people who work with children that do not have specialist qualifications. The checklist is a useful tool to help with early identification.

A cluster – more than 6 characteristics – is an indicator that a learning difficulty may be present and requires further investigation.

Appendix B

Reading Task

Rea ngi eryq icu tas rb plew h arni iff lti

pi sav iff lt kfo eo it le ngb icu es

Th ayu 70b ce eod itha arn gpi il ves ek bofv

eys qto er ntofd lew le in sad ityha om in isu

albr lem te obl ved ectv ond hei rai oes oce hat

op Of nde eha erf isi utt rd nd ntqr ssw

the esow su roc ngdr emsa ryc nan esea ot

yse ellVi alq essi opl reve ommo bth ren

pic qudw ha ma etes ome mes ilpr idw sora he

ke it nor ley tS ti ch ensk orp ppt

ent yar eabi lou me mest is esa ma lo

mwh he era nga bso ti heym slin nb kea tof

ua or te ri un ng cor Th anh evis l pue ng dl

vis lerr sno ddu ngr ni re ds eyc av ua se nci dro

swh ethe tt rbe let sor labp sout or So me il

em er yge heo rof ter syl le of ber met sch

nco ai atw sm Ot ti th re lea areplu bTh

pre mql nth orb ove her mes eya ntc ror rre ey

of nru ei es ot pge ep il ild nwh hidi ese

te dth rey al an ttir eas yCh re oex tth

oql nee os be iou qtom tri Th ar tma nne

dr ems bt eea hav ralo et st ere eno nyi

eal ban ede hin poi glet inp ei rre on

wz an dth stt gto sgoo of on nyou gi

Reading is a very difficult task for people with learning difficulties. They say up to 70% of people with a learning disability have some kind of visual problem. Often people have perfect vision, but their brain doesn't process what they see so well. Visual processing problems are very common, and these are not picked up through a normal eye test. Sometimes children skip words or add them when they are reading aloud, sometimes they miss lines, and make a lot of visual errors noted during running records. They can have visual sequencing problems, where they get the order of the letters or syllables out of order. Sometimes children complain that words move. Other times they aren't clear, or are blurred. They often rub their eyes a lot, and get tired easily. Children who exhibit these problems need to see a behavioural optometrist. There are not many in New Zealand, and the best thing to do is Google to find one close to your region.

Appendix C

Star Tracing Task

Appendix D

42 Characteristics of Highly Effective Teachers of Underachieving Students:

Self-Review Checklist

Aspect for Observation	Yes	Comments/Examples/Evidence
Class environment recognises and celebrates difference		
Multisensory teaching		
Multisensory work completion, variety		
Evidence of differentiated teaching		
Addresses individual learning preferences		
Strategic goals		
Problem solving approach		
Higher level thinking approach		

Structured lessons/ programmes		
Sequential lesson/ programme base		
Brain-compatible learning strategies evident		
Use of repetition and overlearning		
Uses diagnostic evidence		
Teaches metacognitive strategies		
Observes difference and adjusts		
Focus is on what students do right		
Emotionally supportive environment		
Range of visual strategies used		
Differentiated feedback		
Regular verbal and written feedback for third wave students		
Makes use of paired and buddy support		
Uses good software for repetition and overlearning		

Uses teacher aide for repetition and overlearning		
Utilises parent and community volunteers for repetition and overlearning		
Uses multi-sensory / differentiated assessment		
Has accommodations for reading and writing		
Differentiates task expectations		
Work layout accommodates for visual problems		
Provides scaffolding for students		
Is supportive emotionally of underachieving students		
Uses descriptive praise		
Reviews learning at beginning and end of lesson		
States learning intention and purpose		
Has high and realistic expectations for at-risk learners		
Incorporates learning-to-learn strategies		
Engages parents and community		

Curriculum values evident		
A focus on students managing themselves, and their own organisation		
Accommodates underpinning weaknesses		
Identifies at-risk students' characteristics readily		
Refers students appropriately		
Documents diverse student needs well		

Appendix E

Template to Place Students in Various Waves

Gifted and talented students

1st Wave

Students up to 2 years above chronological age, at age, or up to 2 years below

2nd Wave

Students with underpinning cognitive weaknesses – dyslexia, dyspraxia, on the autistic spectrum, ADHD, Auditory and Visual Processing Disorders

3rd Wave

ORS funded, major sensory, intellectual, physical and behaviour

4th Wave

Appendix F

A Summary of Your At-Risk Students

Name	Number of Characteristics on Checklist	Visual Difficulties	Auditory Difficulties	Phonological Difficulties	Short Term/Working Memory	Processing Delays	Gross & Fine Motor Skills	Next Steps

Appendix G

Individual Learning Plan

Achievement Objective	Teacher's Decision to Progress Learning	Learning Assistants will:	Key Competencies
	Accommodations: Strategies and Scaffolding: Planning and Repetition for Rehearsal:		
	Accommodations: Strategies and Scaffolding: Planning and Repetition for Rehearsal:		
	Accommodations: Strategies and Scaffolding: Planning and Repetition for Rehearsal:		

Appendix H

Individual Learning Plan – 10-Year-Old Boy

Achievement Objective	Teacher's Decision to Progress Learning	Learning Assistants will:	Key Competencies
To raise writing level by 1 stage before the end of the year To complete all set tasks consistently	**Accommodations:** To use interests as a motivator wherever possible – particularly writing Differentiated assessment opportunities Minimise writing Focus on quality, not quantity – differentiate work expectations Multi-sensory teaching	Book selection based on interests whenever possible Focus, by teacher aides and home, on multisensory Focus on teaching metacognitive strategies for: Reading Writing Spelling	Using language symbols & texts

To increase work output through on-task behaviour To develop awareness and self-management of strategies which aid and hinder achievement To improve self-confidence in own abilities through the development of strategies	Strategies and scaffolding: Pinging brain/focus brain coaching to curb inappropriate talking Focus on processes Organisation	Teacher aide and home to support in identifying and monitoring inattention or excessive/inappropriate talking	Managing self Thinking
To teach and practice metacognitive strategies for reading, to raise achievement in reading by 12 months before the end of 2016 A developmental spelling programme: multisensory, integrated, reading, writing and spelling programme	Planning and repetition for rehearsal: Tutor Reading/Reading Eggs Lexia/Train the Brain/Jungle Memory Mathematics Buddy Alpha to Omega – dictation words Letter tiles/dice game Weird Word game Classroom resources, etc. Dictation sentences	Tutor reading 3 x weekly with T/A (Teaching Assistant), (20 mins) Tutor reading 3 x weekly through home/community Reading Eggs 3 x weekly (can work at home without teacher reliance) Alpha to Omega 3 x weekly with T/A (20 mins) Letter tiles/dice game at home 3 x weekly with weekly spelling pattern	

Other Considerations:

- **Assess on iCEPT app**
- **Attention to fine motor skill development to improve handwriting**
- **Working memory training**

Appendix I

IEP/Learning Intervention Plan

Name:	Date of Meeting:	Planning Team:
Class:	Review Date:	
Background Information:		

Current situation	Specific Goals	Strategies, Resources and Responsibilities

Appendix J

IEP/Learning Intervention Plan – Year 11 Student

<table>
<tr><td>Name:</td><td>Date of meeting:</td><td rowspan="2">Planning team:</td></tr>
<tr><td>Class:

Year 11</td><td>Review Date:

Termly review</td></tr>
<tr><td colspan="3">Background Information: ________ is on the autism spectrum and has specific learning difficulties, which means he learns differently from others and requires specific learning support. He reports having difficulty with Maths and Science in particular. He has poor processing speed and verbal ability, and some concerns have been raised about his attention and ability to focus. A specialist assessment has been completed to ascertain the need for special exam conditions and to determine strengths and weaknesses to inform educators about his needs. The learning intervention plan has been called for, to allow the team working with ________ to discuss and plan the best way forward.</td></tr>
</table>

Current Situation	Specific Goals	Strategies, Resources and Responsibilities
________ has low self-belief, and a lack of confidence in his ability to learn	Improve self-esteem and confidence in his ability to learn, by teaching and developing strategies to overcome difficulties, thereby improving skills and achievement	All subject teachers, tutors, and mum to teach skills and strategies at every opportunity, focus on strengths and achievement
________ currently lacks independence and has poor strategies and organisation for achievement	Develop successful learning strategies to become a more independent learner	Class teachers and support tutors to teach metacognitive strategies, organisation, and learning; to teach strategies at every opportunity
________ has low-average broad reading skills, which affects his comprehension and subject achievement	Begin a home-reading audio programme, where he can listen and read along with text	Mum will download books of interest on the kindle and begin a nightly reading programme
________ has had a specialist assessment which shows he has processing delays and would benefit from visual perception training	Tutor to teach *Key Comprehension* series, L2	Specialist to include comprehension teaching into weekly tutoring programme
The specialist assessment makes recommendations for Special Assessment Conditions (SAC)	To use Luminosity programme to improve processing speed and visual perception	Mum will download Luminosity and organise 3–4 sessions a week of extended computer time on it. Specialist will set him up on this once downloaded
The specialist assessment makes recommendations for classroom accommodations to assist ________	A SAC application for extra time, separate accommodation, and reader to be completed	SENCO to complete the assessment and application
________ reports having most difficulty in Maths and Science	To ensure that recommendations are put in place where possible to assist/raise achievement	Jenny Tebbutt will write a brief list of strategies and recommendations (attached) which SENCO will distribute to subject teachers
	To ensure that support strategies are set up in these subject areas by connecting a private tutor and subject teachers via email	Maths and Science teachers will email private tutor with any concerns or areas where additional work is required. The tutor may also email staff with questions for tutoring
	An appropriate academic programme for Year 12 year to be planned	This meeting recommends the best academic programme for ________ in 4 academic areas, with Music and Art to balance out the programme
	Maximum achievement for school year to be achieved	

Appendix K

Make the Learning Journey Explicit

To Identify:	**Answer:**
Identify a student you work with. Record aspects of the student's learning needs that you have noticed and wish to adjust. Barriers to Learning:	
What will I do differently tomorrow:	
Accommodations I will make to assist overcoming barriers:	
Strategies and scaffolding techniques:	
Opportunities for repetition and rehearsal:	

Glossary of Terms

Attention Deficit Hyperactivity Disorder (ADHD) – A condition characterised by inattention, impulsivity and hyperactivity. There are three types of ADHD – hyperactive, inattentive and mixed.

Auditory Closure – The ability to use information such as a word, phrase, sentence, or message to construct a whole idea.

Auditory Discrimination – The ability to hear the similarities and difference between sounds, letter patterns and words.

Auditory Figure Ground – The ability to extract the important or wanted information from other auditory information.

Auditory Memory – The ability to retain or remember information that is heard.

Auditory Processing Disorder – The brain's difficulty with processing information that is heard, despite a person having good hearing.

Auditory Sequencing – The ability to order information that is heard.

Auditory Sequential Working Memory – The ability to retain and hold information in memory in the correct order when information is heard, for as long as needed.

Autism Spectrum Disorder (ASD) – A complex developmental condition affecting communication, social and emotional skills, ranging in severity from mild to severe. Asperger's is now included on the ASD spectrum.

Dyslexia – Primarily recognised as a language disability that affects reading, writing, and spelling that is not related to general intelligence.

Dysnomia – The inability to retrieve words when needed.

Dyspraxia – A neurological disorder primarily affecting planning and movement and the ability to transfer ideas from brain to paper.

Fine Motor Skills – Activities that require smaller muscle movement.

Grapheme – A written character that represents a sound (phoneme).

Gross Motor Skills – Skills or activities that require larger muscle movement in a co-ordinated way.

Lexical Retrieval – The ability to find the word required for speech.

Metacognition – Thinking about thinking. The teaching of explicit thinking skills and strategies.

Multisensory – Working with one or more of the modalities – auditory, visual, and kinaesthetic.

Phoneme – The smallest unit of sound that distinguishes one word from another.

Phonetic Perception – Understanding a message that is communicated.

Phonological Awareness – An understanding of phonemes and letter patterns. A range of skills needed to read and spell effectively.

Phonological Decoding – The ability to decipher and read words through knowledge of sounds and letters.

Proprioception – The awareness and ability to hold and use muscles, and balance appropriately to undertake physical tasks efficiently.

Processing Speed – The time taken to complete a mental task or activity. Generally discussed in terms of the average time taken to complete a task or activity.

Short Term Memory – The ability to retain information for immediate use.

Short Term Verbal Recall – The ability to retrieve verbal information for short-term use.

Visual Closure – The ability to complete an unfinished seen picture. An ability to see the whole picture or idea when only shown a part.

Visual Discrimination – The ability to see similarities and difference between letters, words and symbols, pictures, and objects.

Visual Figure Ground – The ability to focus and find the important information from other seen information.

Visual Memory – The ability to remember what one has seen.

Visual Sequencing – The ability to read and write information in the correct order from what is seen.

Visual Sequential Working Memory – The ability to remember and utilise what one has seen in the appropriate order.

Visual Scanning/Tracking – The ability to read accurately from left to right without missing words or lines: to efficiently focus on an object as it passes through the visual field.

Working Memory – The ability to retain information long enough to use it.

Further Opportunities for Professional Development with Raising Achievement

Jenny is passionate about ensuring all educators have comprehensive training in working with students with learning differences to provide equity in education and improve outcomes for diverse learners. To achieve this goal Jenny has developed online development programmes for Learning Support Co-ordinators / Special Education Needs Co-ordinators and teachers to be mentored in their development in at-risk student education. She believes that it takes a minimum of 12 months study to develop the skill set in this area that every teacher worldwide needs to have.

Jenny Tebbutt and her Raising Achievement team travel throughout New Zealand and Australia extensively providing seminars and whole school development. Their programmes include:

- **Career Mentoring**
- **School leader development – Learning Support Co-ordinators (LSCs) and Special Education Needs Co-ordinators (SENCOs)**
- **Teacher development programmes**
- **Teacher aide development programmes**
- **Seminars for parents.**

Both online and face-to-face courses are available. Further information about these are available on the Raising Achievement website: www.raisingachievement.co.nz

Learning Support Co-ordinators (LSCs) & Special Education Needs Co-ordinators (SENCOs)

Online Development Programme: Setting up for Success

Two–part online course specifically designed to support & mentor those in the role:

Part 1: Policy, Practice and Setting up for Success

- **Draft policy and practice to lead school-wide focus on raising achievement**
- **Refine the role to address priorities and responsibilities**
- **Lead a school self-audit analysing the current position and determine goals**
- **Draft a timeline and implementation plan to suit individual school needs**
- **Screening assessments – Identifying at-risk student groups/undiagnosed students**
- **Analysis of screening data**
- **Planning for success – reporting to management/ board, policy sign off**

- **Selecting programmes for implementation**
- **Programme preparation, targeting students and tutors.**

Part 2: Programmes, Resources and Specialist Teaching

- **Programmes for at-risk students: Tutor reading, Tutor Writing, Oral Language, Spelling and Numeracy**
- **Understanding underpinning cognitive weaknesses**
- **Differentiated teaching, and supporting classroom teachers to accommodate learning differences**
- **Understanding at-risk learner needs and teaching strategies**
- **Individual and small group teaching**
- **Monitoring, reporting and evaluation.**

Included in the package:

- **Access to the online programme for one year following registration**
- **Mentoring and email support**
- **Attendance at a face-to-face seminar run closest to your region.**

Register online at: www.raisingachievement.co.nz

Differentiated Teaching Online Programme

Setting your School up for Success

This online course is specifically designed to support and mentor teachers to:

- **Understand and identify the needs of all learner types**
- **Undertake screening assessments to determine which students have additional learning needs**
- **Understand underpinning cognitive weaknesses and how these affect student achievement**
- **Develop knowledge of accommodations and what supports can be put in place for students with identified needs**
- **The 7 key needs of at-risk learner groups and how to implement them**
- **Differentiation, programmes, resources and teaching strategies**
- **Individual and group learning plans**
- **Monitoring achievement: Pre-tests – quality intervention – post-tests**

This course is for all teachers to enhance classroom practice, identify at-risk learners and raise achievement for all learner groups. Learn how to understand and support children with dyslexia, dyspraxia, children on the autism spectrum, children with ADHD and those with visual and auditory processing disorders. The course focuses on teaching for diversity which includes the needs of Maori and Pasifika as well as supporting learners with English as their second language. Differentiated teaching supports all learner groups in classrooms.

Classroom teachers have a year to complete the course at their own pace. 2–3 hours additional work per week can be expected alongside your normal classroom teaching role. Course content is delivered through the online platform, worksheets and practical activities. Each participant will be focusing on the needs of students in their class and implementing programmes, strategies and resources to meet those identified needs.

Register online at: www.raisingachievement.co.nz

Further contact:

Jenny Tebbutt

admin@raisingachievement.co.nz

www.raisingachievement.co.nz

Additional resources available electronically on request.

Author Bio

Jenny Tebbutt was born in England. At 5 years old she said, 'I am going to be a teacher and marry a farmer.' In 1971, at the age of 9, her family immigrated to New Zealand. She travelled to the other side of the world to find her farmer and become a teacher.

She gained her Diploma in Teaching at Hamilton Teachers College at the age of 22 and went on to complete her Bachelor of Teaching much later, at age 40, at Waikato University.

Jenny said she took until she was 40 to become an 'A' level student, realising much later in life that her own challenges with education and growing up came as a result of having undiagnosed ADHD of the inattentive type.

After the birth of her second child, her passion for understanding learning difficulties grew, when he was diagnosed with Dyslexia and ADHD. Being a trained teacher and not having the skills to help your own child with learning was frustrating and surprising, she says.

Jenny recognised quickly that the education system isn't equipped to meet the needs of quite a large group of learners. She gained a specialist teaching qualification from SPELD New Zealand, and a Post Graduate qualification in Literacy from Massey University, and embarked on a career pathway as a specialist teacher.

Working as a SENCO, she developed policy and practice to begin to make change. She has worked both locally and nationally on the SPELD New Zealand Executive, to support change at a national level.

She formed her own company, Designer Education, in the '90s to support schools and organisations with at-risk students. She also spent some time with the not-for-profit organisation, ADHD Rotorua, where she and a colleague evolved the organisation to become the Education and Achievement Association.

Jenny currently works throughout New Zealand and Australia as an Educational Consultant, running her company, Raising Achievement, and delivering seminars and training to schools and teachers. She is driven by seeing positive change in the education sector for diverse learners before she retires, which she says won't be anytime soon.

www.ingramcontent.com/pod-product-compliance
Lightning Source LLC
Chambersburg PA
CBHW021832110526
R18278100001B/R182781PG44588CBX00002B/3
* 9 7 8 1 9 2 2 6 9 1 0 2 6 *